50¢

Themi Vasils and Theodora Vasils
have also translated

Symposium
BY NIKOS KAZANTZAKIS
(Thomas Y. Crowell and Company, N. Y., 1975)

JOURNEYING

NIKOS KAZANTZAKIS

JOURNEYING

TRAVELS IN ITALY, EGYPT, SINAI, JERUSALEM AND CYPRUS

TRANSLATED BY THEMI VASILS
AND THEODORA VASILS

LITTLE, BROWN AND COMPANY
BOSTON – TORONTO

FIRST ENGLISH LANGUAGE EDITION

T 02/75

The translators are grateful to Harcourt Brace Jovanovich, Inc.,
for permission to reprint the poem "The God Forsakes Antony," from
The Complete Poems of Cavafy, translated by Rae Dalven, copyright
1948 by Rae Dalven.

LIBRARY OF CONGRESS CATALOGING IN PUBLICATION DATA

Kazantzakēs, Nikos, 1883–1957.
  Journeying.

  Translation of v. 6 of Taxideuontas.
  Includes bibliographical references.
  1. Kazantzakēs, Nikos, 1883–1957. 2. Mediterranean region — Description
and travel. I. Title.
PA5610.K39Z5213 1975   889'.8'3203   74-22148
ISBN 0-316-48390-7
ISBN 0-316-48391-5 pbk.

Designed by Barbara Bell Pitnof

Published simultaneously in Canada by Little, Brown & Company
(Canada) Limited

PRINTED IN THE UNITED STATES OF AMERICA

In preparing the English translation we have used the first edition of Kazantzakis' final revised manuscript of *Journeying*, published in Athens in 1961. We have attempted to remain as faithful as possible to the original Greek text and have followed its general format, including paragraphing and capitalization in most cases. Where English equivalents were inadequate, certain Greek words have been retained in the text and defined in the notes.

ACKNOWLEDGMENTS

We are indebted to Mrs. Helen Kazantzakis for her invaluable assistance in the preparation of this translation. We also owe a debt of gratitude to the many kind devotees of Kazantzakis who contributed so generously of their time and knowledge: to the Reverend Evagoras Constantinides, upon whom we relied for advice and information on various portions of this work; to our mother, Mrs. Julia Vasils, for her knowledge of idiomatic words and phrases; to Mr. Theodore Tsoukalas for his help and encouragement; to Mr. Vasili Sylaidis for help with certain obscure passages; to Mr. Joseph Bachrach of the Hebrew Theological College for his assistance on Hebrew research; and to Mrs. Evelyn Hansen for generously contributing the library on Egyptian literature and history of her late husband, Leroy Hansen, who, inspired by Kazantzakis in life, shares his epitaph in death.

FOREWORD

The travel journals compiled in *Journeying* were orig-
nally written by Nikos Kazantzakis in 1926 and 1927 for
the Athenian newspaper *Eleftheros Logos*, which had com-
missioned him to visit the Holy Land at Easter of 1926,
and Egypt in February of 1927. Accounts of his 1926 trips
to Italy, Cyprus and Palestine were also published in the
Greek newspapers that same year.

The first edition of *Journeying* was published in Alexandria in 1927. Kazantzakis disliked this edition which, in
the words of Mrs. Helen Kazantzakis, was "dreadfully un-
Kazantzakian." It had been published in the *katharevousa*,
or purist Greek language, the formal, stiff language of the
newspapers. When Kazantzakis' complete works were being compiled for publication, he rewrote *Journeying*, re-
placing the artificial-sounding katharevousa with the more
earthy demotic Greek, making additional revisions, and add-
ing the Morea portion. The new revised edition was published in Greece in 1961, after the writer's death. The journals in this translation are from this last revised edition.

Of special interest to the modern reader is the prophetic
vision with which Kazantzakis viewed these lands. As
early as 1927 he saw the fate of the West shifting to the
East, and the emergence of Egypt as a prominent power
in the world.

The journals, written in the first person, direct, original, fresh — at times awkward, precisely because no art form is intended here — are simple, immediate impressions, synthesized with an acute awareness of History. They show us an Egypt in the middle twenties, while the seeds of rebellion are germinating in a people traditionally docile and submissive to their masters. In describing the Arab fellah hauling water from the Nile with the same primitive bucket of his ancestors, Kazantzakis shows us an Arab inseparable from his past. Similarly, when recording his impressions of a visit to a modern Zionist agrarian community, he describes a vigorous contemporary Jewish generation that is inescapably linked with its tragic Jewish fate. His description of the immediate reality is seldom outside the context of "historical necessity." He sees these lands and people with sweeping vision, fused in a continuum of past and present, shaping their future, preparing for the age to come — the age of revolution.

Parallel with the charmingly simple descriptions of the visible palpable world is the contemporary reality beneath the surface — the awakening of the Eastern masses. *"Slowly but surely, the formidable unity of the Moslem people is beginning to materialize . . . from Morocco to China, from Turkestan to the Congo . . . the Eastern peoples are widening their strides."*

Similarly, parallel with the idyllic descriptions of Jericho, Hebron, Samaria, Galilee, or that modern Zionist miracle, the agrarian commune, there lurks the omnipresent Arab threat, and the fated Diaspora.

Kazantzakis forebodingly sees the Zionist dream ending in tragedy. He sees the Diaspora as the historical necessity that forged the Hebrew race against its will into the leaven of the earth, forcing it to play a special role in History, to save man from his contrived efforts at contentment. It is an eloquent and impassioned argument for those who would courageously keep questioning and challenging the self-deluding contrived equilibrium of the status quo, a theme explored further in his observations on the birth of heroes, and a theme that was developed and expanded later in the brilliant and powerful novel *The Last Temptation of Christ*.

The journals' unique value lies in these firsthand observations of places and people that became major themes in so many of his later works, most notably in the semiautobiographical work *Report to Greco*, which draws repeatedly from the brilliant description of Sinai. Inspiration from Sinai recurs again and again in such works as *The Last Temptation of Christ*, *The Greek Passion*, and *Freedom or Death*. His travel experiences are echoed in most of his major works, in the contemporary Odysseus, and in that intrepid modern-day Moses who carries the new Decalogue, *Zorba*, to name but a few.[1] They helped shape his philosophy, which he capsulized in the *Saviors of God*, and in the *Symposium*,[2] a lost early work recently discovered.

Travel was an invaluable, if not indispensable, source of creative inspiration for Kazantzakis. The East, especially, had a magnetic attraction for him. As a Cretan, he felt an affinity to this part of the world and liked to believe his ancestors had Bedouin blood. The journals in this collection, more than any others, inspired a major portion of his life's work.

THEODORA VASILS

Oak Park, Illinois
February, 1974

CONTENTS

PROLOGUE

THE TIGRESS, MY
FELLOW TRAVELER

The creator wrestles with a hard, invisible essence that is superior to him. And the greatest victor emerges defeated because our deepest secret — the only one worth telling — always remains untold. It can never submit itself to the material boundary of Art. We rage at every word. We see a tree in bloom, a hero, a woman, the star of Dawn, and we cry "Ah," and our heart can hold nothing more. When we try to analyze and convert this "Ah" into thought and art, to communicate it to others, to save it from our own corruption, how cheap it becomes in brazen, painted words, full of empty air and fantasy!

One night I had a dream. I was bent over a mound of papers writing, writing, writing . . . I was panting as though I had been climbing a mountain — struggling to save, to be saved, battling with the words, fighting to subdue them. I could feel them jumping around me wildly, resisting like mares.

Suddenly, bent over as I was, I felt a glance piercing the core of my skull. Startled, I raised my eyes: there, before me, stood a dwarf with a black beard that fell to the floor; he was shaking his heavy head slowly and staring at me with contempt. Terrified, I lowered my neck to the yoke again and continued to write. But the stare kept boring into the top of my skull relentlessly. I raised my eyes once more, trembling, and the dwarf was still there, shaking his head at me with sorrow and scorn. Suddenly, for the first time in my life, revulsion welled up in my spleen, outrage at these papers, books and inks in which I was lost — at my unholy struggle to encase my spirit in beautiful molds.

And with this nausea in my entrails, I awoke. A stern voice rose from within, as though the dwarf were still standing before me and speaking:

"Your life has been wasted in experiments. At the end of every road Victory stands and waits. Yet you, always hasty, lose heart and turn back. The masses do not see the Sirens. They do not hear songs in the air. Blind, deaf, stooping, they pull at their oars in the hold of the earth. But the more select, the captains, harken to a Siren within them — their spirit — and royally squander their lives with her. What other value do you think life has? The wretched hear the Sirens and do not believe. They are filled with prudence and cowardice, weighing the Yes and the No with a gold florin scale all of their lives. And they die. And God, not knowing where to put them — that they not adorn Hades, or defile Paradise — commands that they be hanged upside down in the air between corruption and incorruptibility.

"You are miserably deficient and I am ashamed to drag you along with me!"

"I reached the end," I flung back, "and at the end of every road I found the abyss."

"You found your own unworthiness to advance! Abyss is what we call anything we cannot bridge. There is no abyss. There is no end. There is only the spirit of man, and this spirit names everything according to its own bravery or cowardice. Christ, Buddha, Mohammed found the abyss, but they cast a bridge and crossed over. And

4

with them cross the human flocks. They are the shepherds. They are the heroes."

"One becomes a hero through God; another through his own struggle. I struggle!"

"Hero? But hero means discipline to an order superior to the individual. And you are still beset with restlessness and indolence. You cannot subdue the chaos within you and create the integral word. And you justify yourself whimpering: 'The old forms cannot contain me!' But advancing in Art, you could reach the heroic frontiers where there is room for ten spirits like yours to work with ease! In seeking the truth, even though it is imperfect and human, you could conquer natural powers in order to find and formulate laws which will broaden the circle of our freedom on earth. Even from the expired symbols of religion, you can gather impetus for your own divine attempts and give a contemporary form to the eternal passion of God and man."

"You are unjust. Your heart knows no mercy. I heard you again and again, O' hateful, merciless voice, at every crossroad where I stood to make a choice."

"You will hear me always at your every retreat."

"I never retreated. I always move forward, abandoning everything I cared for, tearing my heart."

"Until when?"

"I don't know. Until I reach my summit. There I will rest."

"There is no summit. There is only height. There is no rest. I despise your body, your soul, your brains. I cannot bear it any more. I no longer want to travel with you."

This merciless voice — the TIGRESS, MY FELLOW TRAVELER — though she hated me, was my companion

on all my journeys. We saw everything together. We ate
and drank, the two of us, at the tables of foreign lands.
We suffered together. Together we enjoyed mountains,
women, thoughts.

And, when loaded down with the spoils, covered with
wounds, we return at last to our cool, quiet cell, this tigress
silently fastens herself to the top of my head. This is her
roost. She spreads herself taut around my skull, digs her
claws into my brain, and we reflect on all we have seen
and all we have yet to see. We're joyful, the two of us,
that all of this world, visible and invisible, is an indissol-
uble secret, deep, inconceivable, beyond the mind, beyond
desire and certainty. We talk, the two of us — the Tigress,
my fellow traveler, and I — and we laugh that we are so
hard, so tender, and insatiable, and know that for certain
one night we will dine on a handful of earth and be satisfied. And when we are in high spirits, or in bitter unbearable grief, we play at setting a trembling God to chanting
pathetic hymns to poor, miserable man.

My God, what joy this is, to live and see and play with
the great Tigress and be unafraid!

And to get up one morning and say:

"Words! Words! There is no other salvation! I have
nothing in my power but twenty-four little lead soldiers.
I will mobilize. I will raise an army. I will conquer death!"

And you well know that death is unconquerable. But the
worth of man is not in Victory but in the struggle for Victory. And harder yet, you know that it isn't the struggle
for Victory either. The worth of man is this alone: to live
and die courageously, disdaining reward. And also this,
the third, the even more difficult: the certainty that there
is no reward to fill you with joy, pride and valor.

ITALY

SAINT FRANCIS

The first countenance that awaited me in Fascist Italy was full of humility and love: Saint Francis of Assisi. I had left Spain hurriedly to be present at the great celebration of his Seven Hundredth Anniversary. Mussolini had proclaimed this day a national holiday; the devotee of poverty, obedience and chastity was enlisted in the Black Shirts, and journalists and philosophers were undertaking the task of discovering Franciscan virtues in the new Fascist battalions.

Thousands of men and women were going by foot, others by automobile and cart along the uphill road from the depot to the charming little town. The dust rose thickly and the air smelled of gasoline. A pale young woman in an automobile took out her purse and touched up her lips a bright red before entering Assisi to worship the saint.

I climbed the familiar, beloved road with deep emotion. Assisi gleamed in the sun, high atop the hill. I recognized the Great Monastery of Saint Francis to my left and the church of Saint Clara to my right, and over the din of the automobiles' roaring I was able to distinguish the deep, sweet sound that spilled from the bells of San Ruffino.

Two years ago, here in Assisi, I had rejoiced for many months in the mystical sweetness of Franciscan humility.

Occasionally an Englishwoman or an American would jar the quiet. But they would soon leave and the simple country of the "husband of poverty" continued its tranquil dream above the silent olive groves of Umbria.

Today, charming Assisi is unrecognizable, altered. Two million worshipers have passed over her in the last three months.

All the homes have been turned into hostelries, the virtuous residents have become greedy merchants, and the girls wear their skirts above their knees.

With difficulty I push aside the crowds to pass. Young men go by in black shirts with short clubs looped over their arms, their black caps cocked and the tassle waving threateningly on their forehead. The walls are covered with the face of Il Duce, fierce, full of obstinacy, with that enormous jaw.

Well-groomed monks, freshly made-up women, dry flat-chested Englishwomen, apish Americans, cardinals in mauve silks, carabinierie with the wings of the cock, young provincial common women, still awkward at plying their trade, having just begun during the opportune holiday of the saint. "Blessed be thou, Lord, for sister Whore!"

I reflect as I force my way through the gaudy crowd: What place does Saint Francis have in Fascist Italy? What place does he have in our contemporary life? A deep exasperation stirs the man who looks at this shameless festival with clear eyes, not because our age is so contrary to the Franciscan ideals, but because it does not have the honesty to admit it. Our deceit, our hypocrisy, our cowardice fill the heart with bitter gall.

I sit in the small square of Assisi opposite the corner where the saint's paternal home stood and I ponder over all his spiritual, quixotic journey. When he started to

preach in this agora — in April of 1207 — the street ur-
chins took after him, pelting him with stones and mud and
he, the town's noble son, was dancing in the middle of the
square, before his angry father, and shouting: "I want to
build a church; whoever gives me a stone, God will reward with a gift; whoever gives me two stones, God will
reward with two gifts; whoever gives me three stones,
God will reward with three gifts!"

Everyone laughed, and he laughed with them. "What are
we," he would shout joyfully, "but the jesters of God, who
were born to gladden the hearts of men."

Little by little, the first companions gathered around the
"buffoon of God." They wandered about barefoot all day
preaching the kingdom of God, with joy and laughter. At
night they gathered in a ravine, in the ruins of a church,
huddling together in the cold. There was no roof to keep
the rain from beating down on them. Yet, in the morning
they would awaken happily and again begin their wandering and preaching and begging.

At noon they would sit on a rock in the sun near a
spring and eat the dry crusts and leftovers that had been
given them. And Francis would laugh and say: "Brothers,
let us glorify God for giving us the great joy of being
alive, of sitting in the sun and eating bread at the table of
Lady Poverty!"

He preaches: "The supreme virtue is poverty." This
widow of Christ, rejected by every home, wandered the
streets, scorned, and no one wanted her. And Francis loved
her and took her for his wife. Poverty, obedience and chastity; behold the three great Franciscan virtues.

If these three virtues had prevailed, if everyone had become Franciscans, the world would be lost. If, again, Francis had preached more practical ideas, his preaching would

11

not have the madness that alone can transport and save men's souls. The ideal, if it wants to renew the face of the earth, must stand much higher than the power of man. In this rests its secret strength, the pull, the painful straining of the soul to reach it, that formidable lifting upward that enlarges the stature of man.

Francis wandered through Italy preaching the most austere virtues with joy; he built monasteries; Saint Clara gathered together the first sisters; the saint was worried. "I fear," he would say, "that the Devil sends us these sisters." He ordered that the brothers not speak to or visit the sisters. One day, however, he himself was overcome. Saint Clara had been cherishing the hope that someday the saint would break bread at her monastery, Saint Damiano. Francis steadfastly refused, but in a weak moment took pity on her and went.

The sisters spread out the frugal table: bread, water, olives. Francis began to speak. Suddenly the doors burst open and a crowd of alarmed monks poured in — they had seen flames rising and engulfing Saint Damiano and had rushed over from their monastery, thinking Saint Damiano was on fire. But Saint Clara smiled and said:

"There is no fire, brothers. It was Brother Francis speaking."

In time, heavy grief burdened the heart of Francis. His companions began to break his rules: they collected money, loved to frequent wealthy homes, amassed books. One day he saw a young monk, pridefully carrying his own hymnbook. "My son," he said to him, "if today you have a hymnbook, tomorrow you will want to have a prayer book, and you will step up to a high pew and call out to your brother, 'Bring me my prayer book.' "

The love of ownership, the thirst for learning, pride and

12

disobedience, women, all the wolves of evil entered into the cell of the saint. Thus, tormented, with his whole body wracked by hardship, he approached death. But the joyful, lofty disposition did not leave him. Blind, lying prostrate near death in a corner of a garden, sleepless from pain and from the many rats walking over him, he composed his celebrated hymns, and in the morning the monks found him singing and clapping his hands: "Blessed be thou, Lord, for brother Sun. Blessed be thou, Lord, for sister Moon, for brother Wind, for our sister Fire." And when in a little while he was gasping his last breath, he raised himself up and asked that they add to his hymns this verse, too: "Blessed be thou, Lord, also for brother Death."

Tonight, how distant, how unlikely this marvelous tale seemed to me! Saint Francis circulates in Fascist Italy, in the panoply of mutual-hating, carnivorous contemporary mankind, and is celebrated on his Feast Day, crowned with flowers — like an animal to be slaughtered.

We find ourselves in the constellation of the wolves. Saint Francis is a small lamb and we like him — precisely because we are wolves.

MUSSOLINI

From Assisi to Rome — the daughter of the She-Wolf. After Saint Francis I was eager to see Mussolini.

Until now there had been two principal ways that one could see Rome:

(a). Like Goethe; admiring the statues, eruditely reviving the classical civilization in one's mind, gazing with joy upon the ancient ruins in the midst of the houses and living people.

(b). Like Luther; angry, with hatred for the clergy, dreaming of another Rome, all virtue and austerity.

Today, Mussolini has created yet a third way to see Rome: simply to look at today's clamoring, tempestuous, militant heart of Fascism, and not be concerned with either the ancient empire or the medieval papal tiara.

Your first impression when breathing the modern air of Rome is this: Here is a man, good or bad, sincere or pretentious, savior or villain — we don't know; but a man of strength, who compels all, good and bad, theoreticians and pragmatists, like it or not, to take part in the battle and declare themselves his enemies or his friends. He does not permit indifference. He does not allow anyone, where Italy's fate is at stake, to not take part in the struggle and say: "I don't want to fight!" You are going to fight, like it or not.

14

Everyone is swept up in the whirlwind that this man's existence creates. In this respect freedom does not exist in Italy today.

A second characteristic that is immediately visible in today's Rome is this: there is discipline. You feel this from the most minor daily incidents all the way to the hierarchical, clear classification that representatives of Fascism have at their command when they speak about the problems of their race.

Here there is not just the security and order that you find in Spain. There is something more, something deeper: discipline. Specifically, there is a certain rhythm, more spiritual and profound than the simple order and security that can also be a result of an external pressure; here the impetus is from within, it springs from a central, hyperindividual idea of a powerful man.

All those who are in step with the rhythm of the Leader name this pressure: submission to a superior order — that is to say, freedom. Because what else is freedom but obedience to a hyperindividual rhythm? Saint Augustine would say: "My God, then only am I free, when I submit to your will!" Substitute the word "God" with whatever other meaning you consider more contemporary and you will see how profound a meaning this expression has.

All those, however, who are not in agreement with the rhythm of the Leader name this pressure: slavery. Quite true. Because in being compelled to follow a direction that is not theirs, they become slaves.

Now the question: (a) Which direction is the closest to being correct? (b) Do those who believe their direction is most correct have the right to impose their will on others by force?

Mussolini responded unhesitatingly and with clarity to both these questions:

"In order for you to see if my direction is more correct, compare the Italy that was before me, when she was free, with the Italy after me, under the Fascist pressure. You shall judge the tree from its fruits; no other criterion exists."

And to the second question, whether he has the right to impose his will on all those who dissent, he answers unwaveringly:

"Yes. And not only the right but also the duty. If I know — as I resolutely believe — that my country will be saved if it follows the road that I opened, I have a duty to impose this belief of mine. We are going through a critical period. We have no time for falterings, discussions, or courtesies!"

These, then, are the four basic impressions of modern Rome: (a) a strong man exists; (b) discipline exists; (c) coercion exists; (d) he who is doing the coercing believes he has the obligation to push everyone, like it or not, onto the road he opened so the country will be saved.

I was waiting impatiently at the Cicci Palace to see this strong man. He would be receiving me shortly. Pallid men were waiting in the antechamber; women were touching up their makeup to appear before the powerful male. Two tall, lean young men in black shirts stood at the door, indifferent, fierce and silent. I noticed the symbol that so frequently appears on coats of arms: two lions standing upright, on guard.

A sullen Fascist approached me and beckoned; Mussolini was awaiting me. The immense door opened and closed silently and I found myself in an enormous, dimly lit drawing room. I stood for a moment, not knowing if anyone was there. A solitary gigantic terrestrial globe that gleamed in a corner like a giant skull was the only thing that I could distinguish clearly.

Suddenly, deep toward the right, in concealment behind a low desk, I made out a man watching me. I proceeded forward.

I could see him clearly now: long-torsoed and short-legged, hypertrophied head with blunt features, all chin and forehead, all angles, as though hewn out of hard wood. Huge primitive jaw, cold conceited eye. The expression of the face tight and belligerent. Two certainties immediately stirred in me: This man was totally committed; this man was unafraid!

I record with faithful accuracy the fast-moving dialogue. Before I could approach any closer, he spoke. His voice sounded tired, contemptuous, curt:

"What do you want?"

I didn't hear well.

"What did you say?"

His voice became more impatient and hostile.

"What do you want?"

For a moment I was silent, agitated. The idea flashed through me to leave, without a word. But I quickly recovered. I realized that this man had the right to behave this way; courtesies are lesser virtues, unadaptable to such harsh, carnivorous spirits. This man opened a road, he holds a nation in his hands; he has the right to behave as he likes. Quietly, then, I replied.

"I want to see you; nothing more!"

His face brightened. His features relaxed somewhat, softened; he spoke with a little warmer tone:

"Ah! that, yes! But no speeches. I'm terribly busy; I don't have a second to lose. Write what questions you want to ask; if they're good, I'll answer; if not — no!"

17

"I don't want to ask anything. I thank you only for allowing me to see you; and if you wish, I will take my leave."

Mussolini was silent for a moment. He didn't know what to decide. Abruptly he asked:

"Where did you learn Italian?"

"In Italy. I lived in Italy for many years. In the beginning while attending the University of Rome, where I was studying law. Later, on other trips because I loved art."

"Before the war?"

"Before and after. It's been years, though, since I've come to Rome and now I see her as though for the first time. I'm experiencing a curious but not unexpected sensation. Here in Rome I breathe the same air that I breathed with such insatiability in Moscow."

As soon as he heard the word Moscow, he jumped to his feet. His face glowed. I hadn't expected such eagerness and warmth. He reached out his hand as though to grasp me by the shoulder to keep me from leaving, and exclaimed in an altered tone no longer tired and hostile:

"You've come from Russia?"

"Yes, I was there four months to study Bolshevism."

"Well, then I'm the one who's going to do the interviewing; I'll ask and you'll answer."

"Very well."

"How are those Russians?"

"I'll never forget how he stressed the words "Questi Russi"! This expression was filled with curiosity, warmth, anxiety. Like a man who was inquiring about members of his family with whom he has quarreled.

"They're working . . . with a superhuman effort to create a new world. Here in Rome I found great similarities between Bolshevism and Fascism."

18

He turned abruptly and looked at me as though he would have liked to pierce me with his hard, passionate eyes:

"What are you trying to say?"

"This: Here and in Moscow I found the same austere, harsh submission of the individual to the whole."

"Good!"

"The same discipline. The same contempt for the minor freedoms, and the same endeavor to reach the great freedom. I found, too, the same burning enthusiasm of youth. Only in Moscow and in Rome is there true youth."

"What do you mean, 'true youth'?"

"That they are ready to sacrifice themselves for an idea. One principle is the same in both of these capitals of the world: something indeterminate, unmeasurable, that you breathe in the air; a faith and a preparation."

I hesitated somewhat, but quickly thought to myself: I'll say what I believe and let come what may! And I added:

"A dangerous preparation!"

Mussolini was quiet. His face was closed, all attentiveness, bent forward. In time he asked abruptly:

"And economically? How are they doing?"

"Great difficulties. The Russians have not yet found a faith deeper than economic theories. They propagandize materialism excessively. And when the peasant is convinced that there is nothing superior to man — that there is no power above him — then it will be impossible for him to want to make sacrifices."

"True!"

He pronounced this word with certainty and satisfaction. In a short while he said:

"What made the greatest impression on you in Russia?"

"Two things: The upbringing of children and the ingenious, enlightening propaganda for the masses."

19

"And Moscow?"

"It's a city where they don't laugh; they work."

"And the leaders?"

"Admirable. Trotsky . . ."

The phone rang. Mussolini leaned over and began listening for a long time. Then curtly, abruptly: "Yes, yes, but don't overdo it!" and he hung up the phone. Then he turned to me and said:

"Write what questions you want to ask me and I'll answer."

"I have no questions to ask."

"Very well!"

And he gave me his hand. As I walked out, involuntarily I found myself comparing Venizelos[3] with Mussolini. The one had a womanly charm, a magnetic fascination which attracts, a high-strung, passionate, covetous, petty soul like that of a clever and spiteful spinster. The other had a virile roughness, an attraction that does not attract but grabs; something repulsive and at the same time invincible. Mussolini is a masculine Venizelos.

"A power pushes me toward a purpose I do not know. I shall be invulnerable until the moment I reach this goal; if I am no longer indispensable to it a fly will be able to overthrow me." These words of the Great Napoleon fit perfectly the mystical faith that Mussolini has in his mission.

Mussolini has all the principal characteristics of the Dictator:

1. His central core is not an idea but a faith. The thought and the deed are assimilated; they are not two functions but one, indivisible; because they do not spring from the intellect but from faith. Now or never! Behold the cry of History that, always, compellingly, captivates the man of action.

This is the cry of Mussolini. The nucleus of his power is

not in dialectical logic, but in the will. A will armed with the latest weapons. It utilizes the most positive modern means in order to reach its mystical goal — which the intellect does not know or, rather, it discovers it every day as long as the will transubstantiates reality.

2. He is ready to die at every moment. Mussolini lives in a tragic atmosphere. To us who have no faith, to us petty rationalists, all his poses appear theatrical. But to Mussolini they are genuine and he feels them tragically, with romanticism and a profound fever of excitement. An indifferent thinker feels contempt because the critical mind sees only the critical aspect that tragic events always have when we, ourselves, do not suffer along with them. But Mussolini is not playacting in the theatrical moment. He lives, suffers, holds up his will and envisions. Simply and tragically, he took his mission seriously: to save Italy.

3. He feels a power constantly pushing him. He cannot stop; if he does he knows he is lost. It is the most characteristic and most tragic agony of Dictators. It is necessary that they do battle incessantly, and win. They are lost if they stop, if they are overcome by indecision, or if they begin discussions. Machiavelli admirably stated the tragic fate that flagellates every Dictator: "It is better that the Dictator err from excessive force than from hesitancy; because Luck belongs to a gender toward which you must always behave boldly and harshly, if you want to conquer it."

Luck loves the young, because she is a woman and the young do not treat her with veneration.

Mussolini dares; precariously he stretches his bow — Italy. What will happen? If she snaps, his enemies will say triumphantly, "Didn't we tell you?" And their trite souls will crow in satisfaction. If he succeeds, his friends will say triumphantly, "Didn't we tell you?" And their trite souls will crow in satisfaction. But Mussolini functions as though he were an instrument of a power superior to him. Deep within he concerns himself neither with success or failure. He does not operate as a reasoning force but as a force of nature. And whether he succeeds or not, he, alone, and perhaps the dark force that has him in its power and that we usually call "historical necessity," or "Fate," will know how they performed their obligation.

What obligation? To push History with all their strength. Every fighter pushes History forward, regardless of what direction he fights toward. Even if he pushes History back. Because thus, in pushing backward, he causes the life force that is going contrary to him to become stronger yet. The highest obligation — and Mussolini embodies this — is force, vitality, militant faith. Only life's dregs are satisfied and quiet, their present way of life appearing good, correct and honorable to them.

The most profound similarity, then, between Fascism and Bolshevism lies in this: They both fulfill the highest obligation. Both, involuntarily and unknowingly, are true partners. I believe there are three superior personalities today who have the right to mold men in their image and likeness: Lenin, Gandhi and Mussolini.

Gandhi works in the center of Asia, in a dark mass of three hundred million, and awakens the conscience of the slumbering East. That which Tagore seeks with his ideological chamomile — to unify Europe with Asia — Gandhi prepares for, wandering barefoot about India and battling to free the Indians from poverty, illiteracy and England.

Closer to us are Lenin and Mussolini. One is in Europe and the other on the borders of Asia. They open two different roads and prod reality to follow. Every country today, like it or not, is torn between these two roads. Not only every country, but every soul, too. You will say, "But we don't want to be either Bolsheviks or Fascists. Is the middle road lost?"

It is lost. In critical historical periods the middle road gets lost. This is precisely why they are critical. The normal rhythm gets lost. It is necessary — whether you are an individual or a people — to leap. An abyss intervenes between the old world, which saves itself even while it is crumbling, and the new, toward which the postwar economic and spiritual needs are pushing us. We must leap. All those who cannot leap will fall in the abyss.

The similarities between Bolshevism and Fascism are great: the force which both utilize to slavishly subjugate the individual to the whole; the harsh restrictions of individual freedom; the inexorable discipline in economic production and consumption and in political and social expression; the hatred for parliamentarianism and liberal democratic ideologies; order, security, immediate suppression of every opposition. An order without compassion.

But the similarities are restricted to methods; the goals are completely different. Fascism supports and utilizes the old idols — narrowing them even further inside the suffocating Italian boundaries. It dangerously exaggerates the patriotic sentiment and upholds Catholicism. It respects property ownership and fights with dubious means to regulate the class struggle. Fascism is sometimes a revolutionary, sometimes a conservative, and sometimes turns back in the chronology of history. It wants to unite, to harmonize all the ill-matched social interests under the Nation's clenched fist.

Full of anguish, this tragic effort of postwar man conforms and still flows on. The realistic framework in which Fascism operates is what renders the efforts of Fascism so

23

extraordinarily serious. What is this framework? Order, security, the strengthening of agricultural and industrial production, the absence of all militarism; work and perseverance.

What will happen when Mussolini is gone? This is the anxious question that friends and foes alike pose with fear. In my opinion all this ironclad Fascist organization is a nature susceptible of veering suddenly from the extreme right to the extreme left. If we keep in mind: (a) the chaos that a big shake-up of Fascism will bring about from the death of Mussolini, or an unfortunate war, or the frustrations of today's overinflated hopes; (b) the constraint which all liberal, socialist and communist elements are suffering in Italy today and which will explode with unrestrained hatred; and (c) the erratic, overimaginative, fiery and fickle character of the Italian people — then it is not unlikely that Mussolini will be nothing more in Italy than the harsh forerunner of Lenin.[4]

EGYPT

THE NILE

When we were finally nearing the wide inlets of the Nile, and the sea, the *Great Green*, as it is called in the hieroglyphics, was beginning to turn green — an old song that has been preserved for us like a cry from the time of the Pharaohs seized my heart.

We are submerged, like it or not, in the terrible anxiety of our times, and it is impossible today for a vital human being to travel carefree as a tourist. What direct value, then, do the pyramids and the gold mummies and the gigantic temples of Karnak or the granite statues of the kings have for us? And how can we be expected to have the desire to enjoy with simplicity, that is, without distraction, those two wondrous decorative ornamentations — the palm tree and the camel?

At night in the desert, stretched out near the fire, when I tried to listen to the thousand distant mysterious rhythmic breathings of the wilderness, all these romantic sounds were lost next to the cry the inhabited tormented city had nailed in the middle of my heart before I had set out.

We live in an age that has a cry of its own and hushes all the charming voices of beauty and wisdom — voices that are unproductive in the context of today's needs. It is another Egypt that we would have seen before the World

War, that great bloody line that separates in two the era and our heart, and it is another Egypt that the eyes of contemporary man behold today. The war not only changed Egypt, but even more important, *a new eye was invented.*

And so today, as I was looking at the low, rich plain of the Nile, involuntarily my mind suddenly set aside the gold jewelry, the colors, the young Egyptian dancers, the victorious Pharaohs and the monstrous gods. And I heard a voice rising from the sand, like the voice of the fellah, shrill, monotonous — the frightful, primordial and contemporary cry of the anonymous proletariat poet of Memphis:

I saw! I saw! I saw! I saw the blacksmiths before the fire; their fingers gnarled like the skin of the crocodile and smelling like fish eggs.

The farmers laboring with anguish in the fields and continuing to work into the night when they should be resting.

The barber cutting hair all day, going from house to house looking for customers and wearing out his hands in order to fill his belly.

Sickness lying in wait for the bricklayer who labors in the sun all day, climbing the rafters and roofs of houses, and at night returns home and beats his children.

The weaver, impoverished in his workshop, his knees nailed to his stomach, breathing polluted air and having to bribe the guard in order to see the light of day.

The postman who makes out his will before setting out because there is danger of his being devoured by

*wild beasts and men, and preparing to set out again
as soon as he returns home.*

*The tanner with tired eyes and fingers that stink like
rotten fish, spending his life cutting cloth.*

*The cobbler who begs all his life and will even eat the
leather he works on to keep from dying of hunger!*

This is the torturous melody that was rising from all of
Egypt as the sun shone upon it on the morning of our arrival. Had I been traveling in Egypt in the days of Saint
Francis, I would be hearing the human spirit sinning in
idolatry and calling to Christ to save it. Had I been traveling
in the days of Goethe I would be rejoicing in the new
harmony rising from the cool gigantic churches and quivering with exultation listening to the sage voice of the priests
as they initiated the young ecstatic Greece into the mys-
teries of life and death.

But I am traveling at a time when man's soul, enslaved to
the machine and to hunger, struggles for bread and freedom. Today, the cry of the laborer — hoarse from drink,
smoke and hatred — is the cry of Earth. And this heart-
rending cry accompanied me throughout my journey, from
one end of Egypt to the other, and guided me.

Tame, enslaved, fellahlike nature. Her broad, muddy
plain sown with cotton, beans and corn. Date palms, acacias,
prickly pear cacti; heavy sky, dense colors, moisture-laden
air. Well-fed ravens alight and flit about on the tilled
ground. Sleepy storks, like hieroglyphics, stand on one leg
at the bank of the river.

And the fellah, like a piece of the landscape, made of the
same mud, stoops toward the river, raises and lowers the

primeval bucket, draws water, and fills the furrows. Faithful, servile, he continues the motion of his ancestors, now thousands of years gone. Nothing has changed. The same narrow forehead, the same black almond-shaped eyes, the same broad downturned lips, the same pointed sunbaked skull. The same enslavement.

The women, dirty, willowy, with painted eyes, walk down to the river, fill their black earthen jugs, set them at an angle on their hard, covered heads — exactly like the ancient bas-reliefs — and slowly climb the embankment in a single line, one behind the other. And the silver rings shine on their sun-worn slender mud-splattered ankles.

This is how the green fan of the Delta, whose heart is the red ruby of Cairo, opens and stretches toward the sea.

And from Cairo, toward the north, the torso of Egypt appears, lean, uneven like the palm tree. Lying between two narrow green strips is the deep blue artery of the river, and to the right and left of it the endless gray sand of the desert. Red birds flutter over the waters, the sugarcane grows thick, and the plain begins to ripple.

For thousands of years the river has eroded the rocks to open a path so that it can pass sixty-five hundred kilometers from Central Africa to the Mediterranean Sea. Stark, yellow mountains have emerged, and the blue water quietly flows through them and fructifies the barren cursed sand. The air grows parched, the desert sizzles, the people keep getting darker — from wheat-colored they turn chocolate, and finally the all-black races of man emerge with their dark metallic glitter.

The birds grow multicolored — swarms of showy cocks with tall aigrettes and blue cinnamon-breasted swallows. The men grow lean, the women hang rings through their noses, the children loll about in the mud, eating sugarcane.

At sunset the mountains across the way take on a rosy hue. The camels pass, their necks swaying slowly. The fellaheen, dragging their buckets, water the earth, singing. All seems peaceful and contented and nothing is lacking except a romantic heart to be deceived by all this tranquillity.

But behind this mask of serenity I could make out the painful, struggling face of Egypt. All this long narrow strip that blossoms green in the midst of the abominable sand is the frightful unending battle of water and man. Should the combat stop for a single moment, all of these ephemeral adornments of earth — trees, birds, people — would be submerged in the sand. Egypt is not simply, as Herodotus says, *the gift of the Nile*. It is the hard daily wage that this great god of Egypt is forced to pay to man. Day and night, for thousands of years, the fellah labors and struggles to tame the god's wild, reckless power. He rhythmically drains his flood and together with him, and with the sweat of his brow, he creates Egypt.

Of the three great sacred rivers of antiquity — the Nile, Euphrates and Ganges — the Nile is most holy.

It is the Nile that transports the soil and creates the earth; it is the Nile that later covers the earth with its water and fructifies her — it begets the plants, the animals and the fellaheen; in the end it is the Nile that compels men to work together, to organize and to discover the first sciences.

In ancient times its sources were a mystery. The Egyptian priests claimed that it came down from the heavens; they made it a god of goodness, a giant grandfather, stretched out in the sand, his myriad microscopic grandchildren swarming all about him.

Its sources are secret, dark, like the sources of God; its face plays like the star Aldebaran and changes colors — green, blood red, muddy, deep blue. According to an old

31

Egyptian legend three men once took an oath to row south-
ward all their lives to find its secret roots. After ten years
the first man died. Ten years later the second died, and the
water had not yet reached its end. And when the third man
became one hundred years old he lay down like a mummy
in his boat to die. And a voice rose from the water and
spoke consolingly in his ear: "Blessed are you because you,
of all men, have seen the most water. Blessed are you because now, descending into Hades, you will find my sources
for whose sake you struggled so!"

Today the mystery has been solved. The Nile springs
from the great lakes of Africa. Swelling in February with
the rains, it carries the soil from the plains of Abyssinia and
descends forklike, white and azure, to merge at Khartoum,
where it continues to its eternal bed, overflows and deposits
its mud on the sand, and creates to left and right a little bit
of fertile land.

In summer the *khamsin*, the dreadful westerly wind,
withers Egypt. The trees are all dust, the grass is seared,
and the animals and people cannot breathe. The river
shrinks, all life in Egypt is in peril; the desert, ever watch-
ful, stretches out eager to swallow her.

But the snows begin to thaw in Abyssinia, and the Nile
swells and rushes down. April brings the overflowing wave
to Khartoum. The water level begins to rise and joy en-
gulfs the plain — soil, animals, people. The eye can barely
discern the daily rising of the water, and heralds run
through the towns and announce the number of centimeters
it has risen. The earthen blocks begin to crumble, insects
come to life, the races of men shout for joy like herons, the
fish sparkle and play in the muddy waves, and birds fly
over the dense waters in flocks.

The Nile is transformed — it turns green, then it reddens

like blood, and finally becomes muddy and covers the land. It fills the canals, the reservoirs hoard up their treasure, and all of Egypt is like a lake from which the towns and trees float by.

These words were found on a pyramid three thousand years before Christ: "Those who behold the Nile descending tremble. But the fields laugh, the riverbanks blossom, the offerings of the Gods pour dawn from Heaven . . . the heart of the gods dances for joy."

Toward the end of August the Nile rises to its highest point. Then it begins to recede little by little. The joy ends. The painful period of the fellah's labor begins — the plowing, the sowing, the irrigating, the reaping. And at the end, the final tragic visage of this labor: the arrival of the *effendi*, the same eternal face with different names, Pharaoh, priest, feudal lord, merchant, usurer — to collect the fruit from the threshing floors.

The Nile not only begets the land, the trees, the animals and the people, it also begets the laws and the first sciences. Its overflow is not always benevolent; it can, when men do not regulate it, become disastrous. So the people are compelled to organize, to work together, so that they can take the flood into partnership, to raise high barriers to stem its force and store its surplus in reservoirs.

And so the people organize into a community and discover the *hydraulic sciences*. Soon they are compelled also to discover *geometry*. Every year the waters of the Nile, in flooding the fields, destroy the earthen boundaries, making it necessary therefore that each individual's ownership be marked out clearly and recorded accurately in a land registry. In this way, the Nile became the cause for the creation of *Law*, that is, the science of making distinctions.

And because one province is dependent on the other and

33

its prosperity depends upon the properly regulated distribution of the water, the Nile compelled the people to accept an austere hierarchy, assembling all the authority in one political body that would have control over all the water and would distribute it justly — and so, out of necessity, the absolute Pharaonic monarchy was created.

In the rest of the world the rain and floods escape governmental jurisdiction. In Egypt the water is regulated exclusively by the Government. When the Great Napoleon came to Egypt, he perceived this secret, which makes austere political authority so indispensable in Egypt. "In no land," he writes, "does governmental management have such monumental influence on the economic life as it does here. If the management is good, the canals are well dug, well-maintained, the apportionment of water is made justly and the beneficent flood extends to more land. If the management is weak or poor, the canals become blocked, the dams break, the regulations of hydraulic service are violated, the water is pilfered and all the land suffers."

I wander along the shores among the reeds of cane and gaze with reverence and fear on this mute water, moving. Heavy, silent, the Nile stirs, directed by man to fructify, fighting all it can, touching, irrigating, forcing the desert. And it, for a moment, surrenders, opens, bears fruit, begets date palms, animals, fellaheen — but behind the trees, behind the shoulders of the men who drag the water, I discern with horror the glittering eyes of the other, the unyielding desert.

I shall never forget one day, from the crest of Iliopolis, how suddenly, through the cool green leaves of a banana tree I caught a glimpse of the desert very close, glistening like a rose, lying in wait. My heart caught because I knew, sooner or later, this frightful tiger would win. In vain, the

Nile stretches out and fructifies a narrow insignificant strip of sand. For how long? And the wretched people, half naked, drag water, open furrows, plant seeds, hoe, struggle. If for one moment the Nile should recede — and it will recede — all will again fall to the smooth, gray invincible sand.

Justly, therefore, the priests offered sacrifices to the Nile, raising their arms in praise:

> Hail, Nile, incarnated in the earth
> and coming in peace
> to animate Egypt.
> You hide your crossing in the dark,
> you spread your waves to the gardens
> and give life to everything that thirsts.
> Lord of the fish,
> father of the wheat,
> creator of the barley —
> should your fingers cease to work,
> thousands of creatures perish,
> the gods disappear,
> the flocks go mad.
> But when you show yourself, the earth
> cries out with joy,
> every belly rejoices,
> every spine ripples with laughter
> and every tooth chews!

And four thousand years later, the greatest poet of present-day Egypt, Ahmet Beys Sahouke, eulogizes the Nile with equal worship:

Your water becomes gold and you drown
the earth in order to bring her forth
again more beautiful.
Your current flows ceaselessly,
like an eternal law of friendship and love,
and from your embrace the valley receives
a rich life!

CAIRO

This is the East, as we love it — brimming with light, colors, scents, filth, and ashes of countless generations that emerged from the river's mud and dried up like bricks in the sun and then returned to the mud.

On the streets of Cairo I rejoice in all the contemporary human harvest of the Nile: lean and nimble fellaheen, worn out from work and hunger; cunning, well-fed Copts; tall, silent, tightly girded Bedouins, eagle-eyed and proud; fierce-looking Negroes with drooping lips and rolling eyes; women with painted eyes wearing heavy silver rings on their ankles like slaves. And circulating in the midst of this dark, colored humanity that smells of musk and dung the odorless, pale, sick-looking Europeans. In the heat of the Arabic sun their stark-white faces make them look like they've fainted.

A *fellaha*[5] goes by carrying two covered infants in a large shallow tray on her head — like fish. Three Arabs, girded with long *yataghans*,[6] are beating their drums and leading a limping old camel crowned with flowers behind them. And all the while they're singing joyfully and chanting: "Tomorrow this tender camel will be slaughtered at Ahmet Ali's butcher shop. Joy to him who is in time to buy!"

A vagrant runs by clutching a lighted bronze incense burner, wafting incense as he dashes in and out of the shops. By now the sun has reached high noon, the streets have filled with djellabas, the spices are redolent in their deep yellow baskets, the cobbled streets are filled with fruits and with camel and sheep dung. A tall, unveiled whore undulates past, smelling of heavy musk; she lifts her diaphanous *maylahya*[7] to her knee and laughs . . .

Over in a small square an old man is cramming wads of cotton into his mouth and pretends to chew and swallow it. In a little while another man joins him and with his two fingers, like a clamp, begins to draw cotton yarn from the old man's mouth, unwinding it endlessly; and a woman, the third member of this theatrical group, takes the yarn, winds it on her spindle, and begins spinning. And when the old man's mouth is emptied, the collection tray is passed and the spectators disperse.

Primitive scenes — women delousing themselves in the sun; Berbers charming snakes; invalids tying colored rags to a tree, seeking cures; hired female mourners suddenly darting out into the streets, flailing their arms, pulling at their hair, and the corpse in a white turban follows behind them on a high coffin covered with a green cloth.

Suddenly there is the sharp scent of cinnamon, cloves and incense. We have reached the famed covered bazaar where all the spices of Arabia are sold. Sallow youths, grasping huge iron bars, pound away in deep stone mortars. Old men, sitting cross-legged on straw mats, mix the spices and grind the occult ointments in small marble mortars, and the women hover about, half lift their veils, and hawk their wares in low voices — black kohl to paint the eyes, henna for the nails, aromatic oil from Baghdad, rosewater, orange-flower water, musk, secret relics — all the divine accouterments of sin.

Farther down the street begin the small workshops where copper and silver are forged. There the artisans, stooped over, surrender themselves body and soul to their work and with the age-old traditional tools pound out the ancient designs on the metal — mermaids, lions, cypresses and quotations from the Koran.

Next in line in the narrow dimly lit bazaar are the rugs, the silks, the multicolored gems, the historic swords, the ivory and mother-of-pearl. I remembered the treasures of the Caliph Mostanse Ben Illah as described for us in an old chronicle:

"A chest laden with emeralds; one thousand two hundred rings with precious stones; thousands of gold plates with colorful enamels; nine thousand multiformed casks of expensive wood embellished with gold; one hundred cups bearing the name of Haroun al Rashid; a gold chain weighing eighteen *okas*[8]; four hundred cages; one enameled peacock; one cock of precious stones; a gazelle of pearls; innumerable rugs, on one thousand of which the dynasties of the world were recorded!"

A fellah held out his hand whimpering. I turned. Suddenly this vision of voluptuousness and wealth moved, like a mirage in the desert, skipped lightly in the air and vanished. I felt shame. There is no greater sin today than for one to surrender to the seductive intoxication of beauty. The ancient Siren lures and paralyzes our strength; the heart strays and forgets today's holy obligation.

I left quickly. I climbed to the crumbling walls of the city and roamed for hours about the wondrous tombs of the caliphs; sacred, slender mosques, minarets, all lightness and grace, stark white against the dark blue sky. The city below roared like the sea, the sun began to lower, the air took on color and turned cooler.

Now I could see the desert all around the houses, ambushing and besieging the city. The huge rose of Cairo lay open on the sand, drinking from the Nile, and blooming. The air teemed with voluptuousness and death.

At night, wandering through the narrow streets of the old city, I stumbled unexpectedly on a curious suspicious quarter filled with lanterns, women and dirty ground-floor bedrooms.

Bare-breasted women sit, stand or dance at every threshold and call to the men. Their bodies gleam — some dark blue, of Ethiopian vintage, others dark chocolate natives, others powdered and white — the European brand. Behind them, illumined by a small petroleum lamp, a huge bed extends from one end of the room to the other. And in the corner, a small pitcher of water — nothing more.

Above the doors hang the various coats of arms of these wretched women: a huge embalmed lizard of the desert, or an embalmed rat, or a drawing of a crocodile swallowing a woman, a mermaid pressing a ship to her breasts. And now and then a tin sign with the words "For Rent" written in all languages.

A young girl with full painted lips and magnificent almond-shaped eyes is holding a brazier with lighted coals between her knees, toasting bread and eating. Farther down the street a hideous old woman is roasting and selling small yellow crabs — the air all around her smells of the sea.

I pass a fat Italian girl talking with her neighbor:

"And how did you make out?"

"I made two pants and three djellabas!" comes the joyful reply from the other.

The tears welled in my eyes. I lengthened my stride to

leave, to escape. But I kept getting lost in the crooked streets. It started to drizzle. At a coffeehouse filled with men and boys I recognized Saint Anthony of Padua in a large frame on the wall, holding the white lily in his hand. In another coffeehouse there was a picture of Venizelos in conversation with Constantine,[9] and farther down the street, George with Olga.[10]

My head was crammed and buzzing like a city of the East. Colors, scents, men, women, ideas, economic and moral problems — I could feel all the ephemeral turbulence stirring in the river's mud and baking in the intense African sun.

Two criteria, as always, shone within me and imposed a hierarchy on the chaotic vision of human life:

(a). The relative human criterion: I felt outraged that for thousands of years all life in Egypt has been regulated according to the self-interest of a few masters — gods, priests, kings, usurers — who harness the fellaheen to the fields like animals and tell them, "Dig, sow, irrigate, and I will reap!" Rarely over these thousands of years has rage and revenge ever flashed through them as they ponder and chisel out their history in the stones. Nor have they ever banded together to escape from the bloodthirsty kings and unjust laws, or from the harsh gods that they, themselves, carve into the granite with their own hands. Today the fellaheen go hungry and labor exactly as they have been doing for thousands of years, and the women go hungry and sell themselves, and the honorable man's heart breaks, without bringing salvation.

(b). The absolute harsh criterion — that looks all this wave of humanity directly in the eye, heroically and de-

41

spairingly, without being deceived by any redeeming theory and hope.

And then all of this Egypt spreads before me like a colorful, waving patchwork quilt. A miracle, this multicolored anthill of humanity beside the Nile. A miracle, the two narrow strips of sand that blossom green to the left and right of it, and produce food for gods, men and beasts to eat. A miracle, too, the barren, boundless desert, that kills gods, men and beasts!

Nowhere on Earth have I felt such violent and sensual contact of life with death. The ancient Egyptians used to place a mummy in the center of their banquet halls in order to look upon death and sharpen their joyful awareness of the tiny flash of their own life.

An old song of theirs has been preserved on parchment:

> Rejoice in each day. Anoint your body with
> perfumes, anoint your nostrils with scents,
> plait a lotus wreath for your throat and
> for the body of your beloved who sits be-
> side you.

> Bid the games come. Cast off your cares —
> till the hour arrives when they will take
> you to the place that silence loves.
> Remember: from there, no one ever returns!

I, who so profoundly love the Yes and the No, deeply rejoice in the two faces of Egypt — the green and the sandy gray.

THE PYRAMIDS

I remembered the famous painting that portrays War — a tall pyramidlike mountain of skulls. Our heart does not easily accept these brutish works that were created by thousands who labored and died under the lash.

Yet, crowds of glassy-eyed Americans, with gold teeth, mill around the skulls like crows. The women climb screeching on the camels, their silk stockings shimmering well above the knees. They quickly make the classic tour around the pyramids, grumble a little, have themselves photographed, and rush back to Chicago.

A party of Americans has just made a bet with a fellah. If he can climb up and down the huge pyramid in six minutes they will give him half a pound. The wretched fellah, lean, hungry, scrambles desperately up the enormous blocks, leaping helter-skelter between the rocks, disappearing now and then, and finally reaches the top; then lunges back down, in a head-over-heels scramble.

I follow him with agony. The Americans, watch in hand, count the minutes. The man returns gasping, falls in a heap at their feet, and raises his neck, panting. But the Americans have won — and, guffawing, they leave. The fellah begins to cry . . .

"Tell him to grab some rocks and break their heads," I said to an Arab who was with me.

But the Arab laughed:

"Why? The masters are right in not paying him. He lost."

"But why should they laugh?"

"The winners always laugh — don't you know?"

In this ancient air of slavery it seemed to me that this little dialogue shed light on all of Egypt's history. Like a hieroglyphic commentary of hawks, rabbits and severed hands, carved on the pyramid.

I walk along the sandy bank; the sun bores through my skull; the entire desert beyond steams; the air flashes and stirs above the sand. Noon. It is the witching hour when the beautiful daughter of Cheops emerges from the Great Pyramid and still roams about in the imagination of the fellaheen and calls to the men. Her father used up all the wealth of Egypt to build the Great Pyramid, and when there was no more, he sold his daughter to strangers. And from each man she would extract a stone as a gift for herself and from these stones she, too, built a small pyramid of her own! Alas, her pyramid forever appears so small and begs for still more stones . . .

Sensuality, slavery, force, grow so harmoniously in this moist, warm, fertile soil surrounded by the horrendous desert!

Death is everywhere — should they look beyond the green leaves they will see the desert; should they stop working in disciplined order for just a moment the river will drown them; should they but raise their heads to the masters, they are doomed.

The Egyptian, except for rare moments in his History, has never set freedom as an ideal. In his political life he has obeyed the leaders, in the arts he faithfully followed the established rules, in thought, the tradition of the ages.

For thousands of years his great passion was one — to defeat death. To continue even beyond death his same life, unchanging. To find a way to preserve his corpse so that his soul would recognize it and inhabit it again.

His houses and palaces are of mud because they are transient tents, but the tombs are of hard stone because they are eternal abodes. Thousands of workers of immortality empty the entrails of the corpse; they fill him with aromatic herbs and tar; they hang talismen on him and place *The Book of the Dead* next to his body — so that he will know how to answer, what road to take, what exorcism to recite.

In the underground hiding places, on the mummies, on the sacred scarabs, the dead cry out: "I have not sinned, I have not killed, I have not stolen! I have not lied, I have never been the cause for tears in the eyes of anyone! I am pure! I am pure! I have not killed a sacred animal, I have not trod on cultivated fields! I have not slandered, nor become angry, nor committed adultery! I have not behaved improperly toward my father nor the king! I have not cheated when measuring weight; I have not taken the milk from the mouths of children; I have not misdirected the water from the furrows! I am chaste! I am chaste! I am chaste!"

But on the wall of the tomb the pitiless drawing is before him; the forty-two gods around him judge him. The goddess Justice disembodies the heart from the corpse and lays it on the balance of the scale; and the terrified corpse calls out to his heart: "Heart of my mother, heart that was my companion since birth, don't bear witness to my deeds too harshly; take pity on me before the gods of Hades!"

If he is saved, the eternal subterranean life begins. The soul is surrounded by food, furniture, animals. In earlier times the descendants brought actual food to the tomb; later they simply burned the food and the soul was nourished by its odor; finally, they merely drew pictures of the food, furniture and animals. The voice of the priests has the power to bring these pictures to life — the animals, the meat, the bread, the fruit take on life, descend from the walls, spread out on the table, and the hungry soul eats and rejoices. And later, the pictures of the chariots with the horses come down, harness themselves, and take the well-fed and happy soul for a drive to see its fields and its children, and to walk in the beloved sun along the river.

"You go out every morning" records *The Book of the Dead*. "You return again to the tomb at night; large candles are lit at night for your convenience until the sun shines on your body again. They call to you: Welcome! Welcome to your home!"

This thirst for immortality governs Egypt. It regulates its economic, political and social life. It subordinates literature and the arts. It comforts the slaves and gives them patience. Priests and kings utilize it as an instrument of wealth and force.

I listened to this cry of immortality, shuddering. The crude pyramids suddenly appeared to me like stone tents, encamped in the desert of death, guarding the soul so it will not die. In a sudden tragic flash they were revealed to me as tall, quixotic fortresses battling desperately to hold the tiny breath of man eternally on earth.

A marvelous song about death has been preserved for us, chiseled in hieroglyphics:

What is death? Every day I tell myself: Death is like someone who has risen from a grave illness. Every day I tell myself: Death is like breathing a fragrance, like

being in an intoxicating land. Every day I tell myself:
Death is like the moment when the heavens clear for
an instant and a man goes out with his net to catch
birds, and suddenly finds himself in an unknown place!

What is death? It is an upright heart, when her time
has come.

It is an upright heart, when her time has come! This is
how the Sphinx was revealed to me when I faced her today
for the first time, a short distance from the pyramids.

Hewn in yellow rock, stupendous, she lifts her head in
agony above the sand, toward the east, as though she were
struggling to be the first to perceive the sun. Yesterday it
had died and descended into the shadow, and today she is
hoping it will come to life again, to rise all-mighty from the
Libyan Desert and warm the hearts of plants and men.

She is the most ancient statue in Egypt. Four thousand
years before Christ she was still here, towering above the
sand, awaiting the sunrise each morning with agony. She
was painted red. Her lips are wide, sensual, animalistic like
a fellah. There is an air of faith and terror on her broad,
mutilated countenance. Her eyes, wide open, ecstatic, look
with horror on the desert.

When she was buried in the sand up to her neck, this
head must have been frightful, like a harbinger of the coming fate of man. Unfortunately, now they have cleared her
of the sand, freed her lionesslike body and the long outstretched feet and the temple between her limbs. The huge
bas-reliefs on her breast seem to cry out: "Help! You, who
are my son, save me from the sand!"

This is how she has been calling to man for thousands
of years. And man always frees her, but the sand returns

47

again and smothers her. The desert has her besieged, and will devour her. There is no salvation. She knows this and that is why her eyes are so terrified, and why she cries out.

I remember the verses a contemporary poet of Egypt dedicated to the Sphinx:

You've embroiled the mind of men with your riddle.
Speak and enlighten us with the teachings of History.
Are you not the one who saw the glory of Alexander
and the shame of Caesar? Today your eyes see nothing
more than a humble village.

But for a man who was spared these offhand historical and metaphysical questions, the Sphinx is mute, deaf, blind — the question does not even exist (this is the civility and vanity of man), but neither does the answer exist.

UPPER EGYPT

We enter Upper Egypt by train. The mountains ahead gleam naked, rosy-hued, desolate. Close by, on the narrow green strip of inhabited earth alongside the water, shouting Negroes, greedily chewing on sugarcane, are hauling up water with derricks. A little girl lifts her apron and dancingly wiggles her belly as we pass.

The houses of the fellaheen are scattered along the roadside, their flat roofs covered with yellow corn drying in the sun. Black and red shawls hang from the doors of these dark, windowless houses made of mud and straw, where men and beasts sleep together.

At a small depot a dead infant has been left lying in the dirt. Its parents are still working in the field; the man plows, the woman follows behind and sows. The day's labor has not yet ended and they wait for nightfall, to bury it. And the babyish, tiny black body, with outstretched arms and swollen head in the little ditch, seems to be digging in the earth, eager to return to it!

Here the green sheath of the Nile keeps narrowing. Finally, a few steps ahead I can discern the borders. Now and then there's an ample palm tree or a thorny blooming acacia or a thick-leaved flat-shaped prickly pear cactus — the last desperate champions of green life. The heart of man trembles with pride and despair. Everything here takes on a superhuman symbolic value because nowhere, as here in Egypt, can you see so clearly before you that life is a tiny island built on the infinite ocean of death. An island made of water, earth, human flesh and tears, and you perceive sharply, looking at the borders here in Egypt, just how courageous and useless are man's toil and pain.

We have reached Thebes, the Great Diospolis, the Hundred Colonnades of Homer, in the enormous capital of the Pharaohs. Today it is a small town that lives off thousands of tourists that Cook hauls in by boat and by train.

The *Cookanthropes*. They straddle the camels and donkeys, clutching their Baedekers, utter a few inarticulate cries, "ooh," "ah," and rush off. They go into the temples and down to the tombs and look without seeing, in their dark blue sunglasses.

I make my visits to the temples of Luxor and Karnak early in the morning, before the *Cookanthropes* awaken. I move about like an ant, without emotion, under the colossal temples. All this bulk is incomprehensible and repugnant to me.

An avenue, two kilometers, used to join the Temple of Luxor with the Temple of Ammon of Karnak. It was twenty-three meters wide, paved with flagstones, and a thousand ram-headed sphinxes towered to its right and left. The altar inside the Temple of Karnak, where only the king had the right to enter, is a hundred and three meters long, fifty-two wide, twenty-five high and is supported by a hundred and thirty-four columns. The entire temple was ornamented with statues up to twenty meters in height.

The gigantic bas-reliefs depict the Pharaoh as he is stretching the bow; captives, tied by the neck, raising their arms; the gods in the act of descending upon the queens and together creating the heir. Above, the hieroglyphics eulogize this mystic union. The woman says: *"Your essence has united with mine. Your radiance pierces my limbs. Your divine dew has become a royal child in my body."*

And the god responds: *"You are pleasing to me."*

I reflect on the last great dynasties when foreigners were permitted to visit Egypt undisturbed. What an astounding spectacle must have spread out before the simple, calm eyes of the Greeks! They, who had been bred in small cities and who worked joyfully and confined their whole spirit in a tiny physical space — suddenly came face to face with these monstrous gods, and the gigantic columns and the human hordes of slaves who had worked without rebellion, piling massive bulk upon bulk in the struggle to capture the spirit.

Egypt was a dark heliotrope turned toward the subterranean sun, the god of death, Osiris. Her statues, the drawings, the hieroglyphics, the temples, were not visions of beauty, but works of supreme necessity.

The statues were a center of magical power that pulled at the soul of the god or the man whom they portrayed and compelled it to reside therein. That is why the statues that filled the tombs were not rendered in an idealized form but were relentlessly realistic, with all the flaws of the deceased. This was so that the soul would be able to recognize its body and enter again and be saved. The false ornament was a deadly sin.

The priests sanctified the water, washed the statue, anointed it, chiseled exorcisms on it, and made its eyes see, its mouth eat, its ears hear . . .

I boarded a boat. We unfurled a sail, two Negroes and I, and we crossed to the opposite bank of the Nile — to the celebrated Necropolis in the Valley of the Kings.

Ashen mountain, arid, desolate. A deep ravine coils through its bowels, and I submerge myself in it for hours. Twisted, intricate, winding, like the brain gyrations of the god of death. I can taste the ashes deep in my throat. Not a drop of water anywhere, not even a green leaf. Only a solitary gray bird passed for a moment — a hawk — it circled silently two or three times and vanished.

This entire western bank was consecrated to death. They dug deep into the cliffs and buried the mummy — just as we bury the seed of grain — to germinate and take on life again. And now, digging, we find them wrapped in swaddling, with hands crossed for thousands of years, waiting. Kings and slaves, saints and murderers, priests and dancing girls, await their soul.

I enter the tomb of Amenhotep II, who died in 1420 B.C. The heat is stifling. The lights go on and I make out the figures on the walls — falcon-shaped gods, the boat of death, the funeral sacrifices, and the goddess of immortality, who is shown on all the columns baring her breast and suckling the king. There are multicolored plants and animals, and on a yellow wall, unfolding with hieroglyphics, *The Book of Hades*. The ceiling is an azure sky with yellow stars. And below, in the innermost secret chamber, the mummy of the king lies peacefully, still adorned with the funereal flowers.

Deeply moved, I roamed about the tombs of the kings until nightfall. I wasn't thinking of death, but rather, I rejoiced in the life that burst forth from the walls of the tombs, shuddering as it once again felt the light and the two burning eyes that were beholding it and resurrecting it.

All around the dead body, life unfolds itself — men plow, graze, hunt, fish, travel along the Nile; women grind, knead bread, light the fire; others adorn themselves, dance and play the lute, smell a flower.

Lean, pale kings hold the keys of life on their breast. Somber mistresses sit at a banquet, and their naked slaves, tall like lilies, lean over and offer flowers and fruit in their outstretched arms. A dancing girl with thick dark hair bends completely backward and with her hands touching the ground arches her body into a bow. To this dancer the ancient poet sang these ardent words that were preserved on a yellow papyrus:

Oh body that holds delight, sweet is the aroma of your chamber. Your mouth intoxicates, it is sweeter than the fruit of the vineyard, and is more fragrant than a flower garden in bloom. It is better for one to be with you, by your side, than to eat when he is hungry, or rest when he is weary!

Often in these underground burial walls there is a burst of humor, and teasing words. One fresco shows a boatman traveling along the Nile. An old man is on the shore. Beneath is written this brief dialogue: "Come on, old man, walk on the water!" — "Shut up!"

Elsewhere, women are kneading and under the fresco is written: "Knead well! Strength!"

Slaves are washing jugs; they fill them with beer and seal them. And below the hieroglyphics write: "Wash them clean, fill them with cool beer, seal them."

Elsewhere, naked women dance. Others, sitting cross-legged, play the flute. And below is written: "Life is good, the dance is good, song is good."

In another fresco the king is out riding with his seven daughters. In the first chariot there are three: the king, his wife and youngest daughter. In the others are two each of the princesses; the eldest holds the bridle, the youngest leans over and embraces her sister. Behind are many chariots with courtiers, slaves, monkeys, and peacocks. Rich, warm colors, white gowns, plumes of ostrich feathers on the horses.

With what charm, with what seriousness and force do all these shadows ripple in the dark! As though they live and reign far away, and I see them but cannot hear them.

Lithe, painted, with a flower in their hair, these ancient women rise and blossom in the furrows of my mind. And the heavy fatigue of the daily toil, all the dead, torturous labor comes surging to life inside me and righteous outrage chokes me.

I begin to think if I forcibly break through the door of my memory I will remember it was I who sang the song to the dancing girl, it was I who stooped and hauled stones and cried and was hungry, and it was I, one hundred years old, who climbed and climbed with my tiny heart, unyielding against the current of the river.

In descending to Hades I found the mysterious sources of the river, the immortal water; and stretched out in the tomb I drank and my joints were renewed and I ascend again to earth, waving my two arms in the air — like oars. Again against the current.

It was dark when I emerged from the renowned tomb of Tutankhamen. In the cliffs ahead of me the mouths of the royal tombs gaped a bluish hue and the ashen mountain had for an instant turned crimson.

I was tired. I had given much of my heart's blood to bring the dead shades to life and to rejoice a bit, spending my strength in an unhoped-for attempt. Only two of all the shades remained and did not want to leave me. They knew that I loved them dearly — and nothing in the world has more need for love than the dead.

These two shades that followed me all the way from the ravine of the dead to the Nile were King Amenhotep IV (Ikhnaton) and his wife Nefertiti. I have loved few living people as much as this mystical royal pair that lived 1370 years before Christ. The body of Amenhotep was stunted. He was hydrocephalous — with a protruding jaw, narrow forehead, long hooked nose, full sensual lips, thin sickly neck, asthenic shoulders — and the chest, loins and feet of a woman.

But in this deformed man-woman body there dwelled an ecstatic fearless soul. He set himself a purpose: to topple Amon, the omnipotent god of Egypt, from his throne and raise in his place the god Aton — the Sun. He was still a young boy of fifteen when he ascended the throne. He immediately built a chapel of red granite right in the center of the holiest temple of Amon at Karnak, and dedicated it to the Sun. In the beginning the Sun god is portrayed with the body of a man and the head of a falcon. And atop him sits the all-circular fiery disk. But little by little, worship becomes dematerialized — without human body and without falcon. Only the crimson disk of the sun. Rays spread out fanlike, descend upon earth, terminate in the form of arms and caress the body of the king and his wife, Nefertiti.

This representation — the Sun with the long arms caressing the world — was proclaimed the symbol of the new religion.

Oh, Sun, the only god, you have countless arms, you stretch out your arms to those you love!

And another hymn salutes him:

> *Hail, most beautiful daily god! Your rays come — and*
> *we know not how — atop our heads. Gold is not as*
> *brilliant as your rays. When you travel in the heaven,*
> *everyone watches you; when you walk in the dark*
> *mysterious region, everyone prays.*

Amenhotep declared a furious war against the old religion of Amon and his priests. He smashed all the statues of the old god in all the temples and obliterated his name on the hieroglyphics. The new worshipers climbed to the peaks of the obelisks and descended to the dark bowels of the tombs to find the name of the image of Amon in order to break it. Only thus, by destroying his visible body, they believed they could also erase the god's soul.

Tutankhamen, the king who came after him and who married one of Amenhotep's daughters and brought back the old religion relates:

"The temples had become fields and the altars roads through which people now passed. The gods turned their face away from earth. When a god was invoked he no longer came. When a goddess was invoked she no longer came. The soul of the gods had become disgusted with its body."

Amenhotep renounced his name in deference to Aton; he renamed himself Ikhnaton, "Glory of the Sun." He abandoned the city of Amon, of Thebes, and built a new capital near the hill we know today as Tel el Amarna, between Thebes and Memphis, and named it Akhetaton, "Horizon of the Sun." He built temples and palaces, held great festivals, distributed land and high offices to the faithful, proclaimed himself "Great Prophet of the Sun," representative of god on earth.

This revolution was not only religious but, above all, had economic motives and political aims. Ikhnaton controlled all the vast property of Amon. He restricted the power of the clergy and subjected it to royal authority. He proclaimed the high office of the Pharaoh supreme and divine. At the same time he elevated to the stature of supreme god not the provincial purely Egyptian Amon, but the Sun. The Sun was worshiped by multitudes of Asiatics and Africans. He was accessible to all, to those of the same race and those of other races, to the educated and the illiterate — and consequently it was simple for all to acknowledge and accept the sovereignty of Egypt. Amon separated the Egyptians from all other nations; the Sun god would unite them.

This religious and political reform gave a new breath of life to literature and the arts during the reign of Ikhnaton. A revolution broke out in all branches that bred dogmas, rules and traditions. In all the works that have survived we feel a moving emotion and disturbance, a violent love of life, raw candor, warm feeling.

In architecture, the portals were abandoned, as were the dark halls and the altars that were inaccessible to the lay people.

The sun-worshiping Pharaoh, the Apostate, built broad, open temples where the sun penetrated everywhere and shed its light on them; a courtyard with columns in the center of which was the open altar and sacred symbol — the purple-crimson sun orb and its innumerable arms. The dark ceremonies of death were no longer performed. On the tiles of the courtyard, on the walls, everywhere, there are multicolored birds, rivers and fish, gamboling animals, leaves from the trees dancing in the wind.

Statues of the god were abolished; the new god had no body. Sculpture no longer depicted god, but man, and particularly the highest form of man — the Pharaoh. Everywhere, in all the works that have survived from this brief Egyptian renaissance, we discern the long, sensual ecstatic face of Ikhnaton.

And with him always, his beloved wife, Nefertiti. Tall, lovely, exuding energy and passion, with the willful, pointed chin, with the fleshy Asiatic lips. Frequently she is shown completely naked, offering a flower to her husband. There is a small naked statue of her, made of gray granite, portraying her walking heroically with a lengthy stride, tightly clenched fists, neck taut, gaze lifted upward, resolute and despairing, as though she is pondering the desert.

The excavations of Tel el Amarna have uncovered scenes on stone of unprecedented realism. For the first time in Egyptian art the family life of the until now unapproachable Pharaoh is depicted with intimacy, joy and harsh exactness. At times he is submerged in the arms of the sun and you see his body quivering with joy and agitation. At other times he sits on his throne holding his wife on his lap as he kisses her. Then again, he and his wife are sitting together in the rays of the sun, while his daughters climb upon his lap and play.

So strong is the love of nature and love for color and for every act of life in these works that you vividly recall the Cretan frescoes of the same period. And when you consider that in 1400 B.C. the second palace of Knossos was destroyed and the artisans were scattered about in foreign lands you feel it quite probable that the Cretan breath of life blew into this short-lived renaissance of inflexible, sacerdotal Egyptian art.

Abruptly, at the peak of this revolutionary creativity, young Ikhnaton died. We know nothing about his death. Only this: he had ordered that no matter where he died he should be buried in his beloved new capital; but a few years ago his mummy was found at Necropolis of Thebes, next to the mummy of his mother, Tiy. Alongside were also preserved some of the funeral ornaments of the lost sarcophagus of Queen Nefertiti.

All of his most valuable adornments had been stolen; only the embalmed body with the hydrocephalous skull and the skeleton remained.

He left no son. None of his work lived after him. In vain his followers had carved this prayer on the stone: "May your work prevail until the swan turns black and the raven turns white, for as long as the mountains stand and the water in the river does not flow back!"

Tutankhaton (the Living form of Aton), the son-in-law and heir of Ikhnaton, gave up the new religion, renamed himself Tutankhamen, returned the capital back to Thebes, and again restored Amon to the summit of worship.

But the new spirit continued to give life to the arts for many years. When Tutankhamen's tomb was discovered the year before last, men's eyes were dazzled by the gold and the charm, grace and refreshing spirit about the statues, drawings, furnishings and adornments of the tomb. The pale king and prophet left us yet another immortal work. He was a poet and had written a moving hymn to the Sun. It was found in the tombs of Tel el Amarna:

You ascend on the horizon, O Aton, giver of life!
When you rise in circular perfection on the horizon

you fill the earth with your beauty! You are beautiful and great, brilliant and high above all the earth. Your rays embrace the world and all that you have created. You are far away yet your rays touch the earth.

When you descend to repose in the western sky the earth sinks in darkness as though dead. Men sleep with covered heads, and no eye sees another. You can steal whatever treasures they have placed beneath their pillows and they will be unaware. The world slumbers because he who created it has descended — to sleep.

But dawn comes, you emerge on the horizon, glowing. You hurl your rays and the darkness disappears. The earth rejoices; men leap to their feet; you rouse them. They bathe their bodies, they dress. They lift their arms to you in worship. The earth begins its daily chores.

The cattle take pleasure in feeding. The trees and plants flourish; the birds soar from their nests and laud you with their wings. All the wild animals leap up; all creatures that fly and all that crawl come to life because you shone upon them.

The ships sail upstream and downstream; every road opens because you appeared. The fish in the river leap in the air; your rays penetrate the depths of the sea.

You spawn the child in the loins of women, and create the seed in men. You nourish the child in its mother's belly and soothe it so it will not cry, o wet-nurse within the mother!

60

And when the child is born it is you who opens its mouth to speak and you who sees that it eats and drinks.

It is you who blows breath in the chick imprisoned in the egg and gives it strength to break the shell. It springs from the egg and begins to chirp and stand on its feet, because you willed it.

How bountiful are your works! Much is hidden from men; no other god exists than you!

You created the earth according to your heart's desire, you alone created it, with men and animals, with legged creatures that walk and winged creatures that fly. You set every man in his place, you give him whatever he needs, various tongues, various laws, various colors of skin.

Your rays nourish every land, and when you rise all your creatures rise and grow.

You ascend, you descend, you return again . . . You are in my heart!

No other knows you as I do, I, your son, Ikhnaton, who came out of your body; and your wife, Queen Nefer-nefru-aton, Nefertite![11]

CONTEMPORARY LIFE

I return to the brisk modern cities. I saw the shades, I paid tribute to the dead — a little blood — and am redeemed.

At first I had considered not going to see them at all. I was interested in what the living had to say. How today's Egyptian soul was confronting the postwar struggle. This, only, concerned me, I thought. But after the first intoxication with the vitality and noise of the robust face of Egypt, an overwhelmingly sweet and poignant voice rose up from the earth and took hold of me. The dead cried out, thirsted, wanted to come to life, even if only for a moment, inside a heart that was still warm and throbbed beneath the sun.

People who believe in an idea are of three types:

(a). Those who are not troubled by past beauties — because they do not know of them or understand them. They do not hear the voice of the Siren. Without fear of straying, they fight the daily battle narrowly, fanatically and productively.

(b). Those who know and love the past beauties and are charmed by all of life's faces and know that her last face also — today's idea — is similarly ephemeral and relative. Knowledgeable, weary, sensuous, they fold their hands and listen to the Siren.

(c). Those who know and love the past beauties and for

one brief frightfully intense moment are charmed by the old song, but forcefully tear themselves away and continue the journey, snatching up the Siren in their memory. Of necessity they urgently proclaim the relative present-day truths and continue to struggle like the first group, after having been gladdened for a moment like the second.

I return to Cairo, to the vital heart of modern-day Egypt. I rush from morning until evening seeing financiers, politicians, journalists, intellectuals. Men full of fire, guile, patriotism and expedient cleverness. I try to become acquainted with as many as I can. What is the alleged regeneration of modern-day Egypt? How can the Eastern mind assimilate and pursue European ideas? And most important, what postwar fever exists on the banks of the Nile and what is its contact and connection with the formidable, prodigious reality of our age — the awakening of the Eastern peoples?

All Asia — China, Siam, India, Arabia, Syria, Palestine, Turkey — is in ferment. All Northern Africa awakens, the colonial structure of Europe is staggering. What is Egypt's special role in this dangerous, fateful awakening of the Eastern world?

I speak with a distinguished Egyptian intellectual:

"If you are to understand the Egypt of today," he says, "you must clearly bear in mind that the History of modern Egypt is divided into two critical periods: from Mohammed Ali to the European war and from the European war to the present.

"Mohammed Ali is the father of today's Egypt. An Albanian, born in Kavala, he distinguished himself as an officer in Egypt and became Pasha in 1805. He took advantage of Turkey's weakness and in 1840 succeeded in achieving an expansive autonomy for Egypt.

"He had a great soul and enlightened mind. He opened Egypt to European civilization, invited foreign organizers, restructured the army, reorganized education and agriculture, and sent scores of young Egyptians to study in Europe. He breathed a new dynamic life into the land. Mohammed Ali is the Peter the Great of Egypt.

"His eldest heir was Ismail — talented, vainglorious and extravagant. Egypt achieved complete internal autonomy in 1866; as to external matters, she was permitted to contract trade agreements and loans and, finally, in 1873 was allowed to enter into all foreign relations, provided Turkey's political treaties were not harmed.

"However, through his excessive extravagance, Ismail increased Egypt's national debt in 1876 to ninety-one million pounds, and England and France, his greatest lenders, subjected Egypt to economic control. We were forced to accept foreign pressure and our highest positions fell into the hands of the English.

"The people were aroused. Pasha Arambi, a daring, fanatic patriot, organized a revolution and demanded that the foreigners be ousted and parliamentary government be introduced. Many foreigners were killed and Arambi fortified Alexandria. The British navy bombarded the city and landed troops.

"That is when the British occupation began. It did many good things — it brought order, organized the services, and attempted to work out a new economic structure. But the enlightened people always looked upon the foreigners with impatience and wanted to be rid of them and become masters of their own house.

"In 1900 a commanding figure, all fire and intellect, appeared on the political scene of Egypt — Mustafa Kemal.

He formed the National Party, his aim being the 'liberation of the Egyptian nation.'

"Extensive propaganda regarding the rights of Egypt was activated abroad. A congress of the party assembled in Brussels in 1912 and declared the independence of Egypt, and war against the Anglophiles and the Copts, who were then considered tools of England.

"But all this activity and thrust toward liberation was confined to a narrow circle of Egyptian intellectuals. The people, the fellaheen, remained completely apathetic. They were not touched by the abstract concerns of the educated class; on the contrary, the people were satisfied because the English imposed discipline and order and distributed the water justly.

"The fellaheen awakened only as a result of the European war."

My companion lucidly set forth the contemporary problem of Egypt — not only the political and economic problem, but of its civilization generally:

"The European culture that Mohammed Ali and his successors ushered in so profusely is not from the bowels of the common people; it is not an outgrowth of our local conventions and our particular Eastern mentality. And consequently, our culture is now nothing more than an imitation.

"That' s why we haven't created anything, either in science or in the arts. Our only original work is in theology.

"We slavishly imitate Western culture and gape over anything that comes from Europe. We, too, are following the contemporary universal necessity. A new wind blows over all our lives, coming from England, from France . . .

"We, too, have our feminists, our writers and poets who are influenced by Victor Hugo and the Romanticists. We have myriads of translations of European works — in science, sociology, law, fiction, drama.

"Newspaper circulation has expanded vastly, especially after the war. This is due to two reasons: (1) political and economic issues interest a much wider circle today; (2) there are more people who can read now. In 1917 only eight percent of the people knew how to read and write. Today vast numbers of schools are in operation and attendance is compulsory.

"Five hundred students are sent to Europe annually, under the nation's subsidy, to study engineering, chemistry, law and medicine. Our budget records two hundred thousand pounds a year for these scholarships.

"We bring in as much knowledge as we can from Europe. Of necessity, the dilemma for all Eastern peoples is tragic: either they will want to shut out Western civilization — and then remain backward, out of step with modern life, the easy prey of every advanced people; or they will accept Western civilization — and will be compelled to imitate it slavishly, and set aside their own small but yet original economic, social and spiritual life."

"There is no dilemma," I answered. "Whether they want it or not, all backward nations will follow European civilization — its economic structure, its scientific progress, its society and politics.

"There is no other way.

"Only when Western civilization falls and its marvelous structure dissolves will the Eastern world again be able to give to Europe what it always gave: the new seed.

"Because I don't think it's by chance that all religions — that is, all the seeds — that worked the bowels of the Earth come from the East. The East is possessed of madness, and burns. The West receives, nurtures, refines, analyzes — transubstantiates the flame into light.

"Until now, this is how the formidable collaboration — male and female — has been apportioned on our planet. The Easterner is the husband of Europe."

We walk beneath the date palms on the banks of the Nile. We talk, and all of Egypt's dramatic postwar struggle unfolds before me. How, with impatience and violence, a people awakens from its slavery, searches, aspires, drags itself up to find enlightenment and freedom.

The fellaheen have understood their slavery for the first time only since the World War. They sent more than a million souls to the war. Their animals and crops were commandeered; at war, under the lash, forty thousand fellaheen became special laborers and worked for the needs of the allied army.

At the same time a great internal ferment was brewing in the land; the economic and social establishment of Egypt was changing. New small industries were developing, a new class of capitalists was emerging, and the old masters were falling. Parallel to this the special laborers who worked in the army were creating a conscious working class for the first time in Egypt's history. Too, the peasants were suffering horribly from the war — they were killed and their animals and possessions were taken from them. Civil servants were replaced by Englishmen, who were paid generous salaries.

The war ended and the Egyptians waited for England to fulfill her promise to liberate Egypt. England refused. Strikes broke out, extreme nationalist parties were created; elections were effected and then nullified, the people were inflamed; all the land seethed. Fellaheen and Copts united

67

and demanded their freedom; the crescent and the cross joined together at mass meetings and national holidays. Everything that religion had once separated, the national conscience now united. The people passed the first stage of their liberation — religion. They had finally reached the second, but not last stage — the nation.

I was talking to a crafty, powerful Coptic leader:

"There is one way for a people to awaken, and that is for it to become restored economically. Egypt has great stretches of land that belong to a few feudal lords. Millions of fellaheen work on these lands and die of hunger. How do you confront this problem?"

My companion coughed. I repeated:

"What is your opinion concerning the expropriation of land?"

He thought a little. Of course, he would have preferred my not being so indiscreet. It would have been so comfortable and so rhetorical to confine ourselves to the great beautiful words: "Nationalism, brotherhood, freedom, the soul of the fellah!" Why should we speak of his body? He played with the telephone in his nervousness, then let it go.

"Egypt is a very rich land," he said, resolutely. "We have two and three harvests a year. A small piece of land here could easily feed an entire family . . ."

"And so?"

"And so the matter you referred to" — he avoided mentioning the precise expression "expropriation of land" — "does not have the acuteness here that it appears to have in other less endowed lands."

"And so?"

"But I think I have answered your question."

And so he had. I left with a tight heart. The fate of the

fellah, our brother, that unfortunate man and beast who works like a dog and dies of hunger, filled my heart with anguished indignation and bitterness.

The Moslem world is awakening. According to the latest statistics (1923) the Moslems of the world have reached two hundred and seventy-seven million.

Egypt is destined to play a primary role. Her geographic location in the center of the Moslem world, her close daily contact and friction with Europe, and her accelerated political and economic fermentation during the last few years make her the most sensitive and progressive vanguard of the Moslem battle array.

From Morocco to China, from Turkestan to the Congo, the Moslems, as they come in contact with the opponent Europeans, are beginning to realize that the closest common bonds unite them — religion, tradition, economic interests.

Slowly but surely, in spite of obstacles, misunderstandings and delays, the formidable unity of the Moslem people is beginning to materialize before our eyes. So close is it before our eyes that we don't even see it. And when we do see anything, it is only a chance fragment, never the whole.

Mustapha Kemal, Zaghlul, the present king of Hejaz, the new Luther, Ali, the leader of the Indian Moslems and dearest co-worker of Gandhi — all these figures are not simply interesting personalities. They express an internal prodigious ferment. They are the few clear voices that are beginning to manifest the inarticulate, unformed as yet, will of the eastern Moslem world.

And still more. Side by side with religion, a new idea is working itself out and stirring the Asiatic and African peoples: nationalism. The national conscience has awakened for the first time in these people.

Religion no longer plays the major role in their actions; the new idea of the nation now fires them with enthusiasm and unifies them.

Many Eastern peoples awakened, thanks to the World War.

1. By using them as their tools, the Europeans ignited and fanned the national conscience in them. They taught them that they had rights and that if they would help the Allies, the Allies would give them their freedom after winning the war.

2. Millions of Egyptians, Indians, Senegals and Algerians hastened to fight in the European armies. There they were taught how to fight in a modern war, how to utilize fully the latest military equipment, and they were taught even more: to kill Europeans.

3. With daily association the Eastern people came to know the Europeans better. They saw them from close, they saw their many petty motives, the dissensions between them, the collisions of self-interest between them. They stopped fearing them.

4. The war ended. They returned to their countries completely changed, awakened, with specialized technical knowledge, saturated with the propaganda of revolutionary theories. They knew they had rights, and they asked for them. They became the formidable yeast of their people.

5. The Europeans did not keep their promises. Not only did they not give them the absolute freedom they had promised in order to entice them into the war, but out of self-interest they frequently used violent means to stifle the light they saw kindling in the dark Eastern masses.

But light — this is its nature — always augments itself; it bristles and becomes a flame.

Add to these causes the two main factors that awaken and unite the East against the West:

(a). Today, any action anywhere on earth has an immediate repercussion on all five continents. News of a victory of the Eastern armies in Morocco or Shanghai travels instantly, thanks to modern means of communication, to all Eastern peoples and fills them with enthusiasm and faith. This phenomenon is, of course, unprecedented in the history of man.

(b). Russia. She regulates the entire revolutionary excitement of the East and systematizes the activities and the hatreds of the Eastern peoples against capitalistic Europe and America. She propagandizes simple things: that all peoples should expel the capitalists who exploit them, and should become masters of their own house.

Thus, through various causes, the Eastern peoples awaken and foment unrest. As is natural, economic causes play a major role here, too. The necessities of life expanded after the war. Economic conditions changed drastically. The backward peoples, of necessity, widened their stride.

Look at Egypt: Earlier, only foreigners were capable of exploiting her wealth, of operating her commerce, of building factories, instituting banks, undertaking large technical works. Today the native citizens are beginning to replace the foreigners in all these manifestations of economic life, with skillful adjustment. Not only do they no longer need the foreigners but they are a hateful hindrance as well. The new urban class that came into existence mostly after the war has an immediate imperative advantage in being rid of them.

Economic fermentation and the vital involvement of the indigenous native Egyptian element are deeply rooted in the economic rebirth of the country.

Commerce used to be in the hands of foreigners; the importing and exporting of goods was handled only by foreign agents. Today the native Egyptian deals directly with the European houses. He is compelled, therefore, also to adopt European financing methods, he signs bills of exchange — something he would never have consented to before — he builds banks, he modernizes.

Industry was formerly primitive; wood, iron, copper and cotton were worked with medieval tools. Today the natives have brought in European machinery, they have built factories, and they follow all the engineering advancements.

Today they have trade schools and schools of commerce. Transportation methods have changed. Automobiles have penetrated everywhere. The towns are finally joined together and the exchange of merchandise and ideas is swiftly executed.

For economic reasons polygamy among the people has been abolished. Marriages between Moslem men and European women are constantly increasing. Now families of different sects live together under the same roof, and quite often they are Moslems and Christians — something unheard of before. As a result of this forced contact that postwar economic causes brought about, the established customs are altered, ideas change, the mind broadens.

Many Easterners and Europeans proclaim with beautiful phrases the superiority of the Eastern soul and with romantic exaltation declare that the light will again come from the East.

Perhaps. But in order to stand on solid ground and avoid the unreliability that prophecies always have, I think it is well for us to restrict ourselves to impartial verification of today's ferment in the Eastern world and reinforce ourselves with direct, firsthand evidence.

There is no Eastern civilization today. Whatever is purely Eastern is provincial and behind the times — unadaptable to today's life. In order to create again its own civilization the East will of necessity apprentice itself to the West. It must first complete its service in Western civilization. And this service has begun. It has adopted the European technical means of production, the new methods of industry and commerce, the analytical critical method of thought, and it is attempting to adapt the Eastern way of life with European science.

The future belongs to the peoples who combine these two:

1. Modern technology.

2. One faith. I don't mean religion, but generally a central, deep-rooted conscience.

Today Europe has the first. The East has the second. The East, especially after the war, started to be initiated into technology and to become organized. Europe is steadily breaking down, losing every central belief. The new World War that is coming will dissolve her, in all likelihood, totally and violently. And then the fate of the world will shift from the West to the East.

And when I say East I also mean Russia.

CAVAFY

Without a doubt, the poet Cavafy[12] is the most exceptional intellectual figure of Egypt.

Sitting opposite him at a small table in his palatial mansion, I try to make out his countenance in the dim light. The table between us is filled with glasses of whiskey and *mastiha*[13] from Chios — and we are drinking.

We talk of sundry people and ideas, we laugh, fall silent, and after some effort again resume the conversation. I try to hide my emotion and joy behind laughter. Here before me is a total man, who quietly performs the achievement of his art with pride, the hermit chieftain who subjugates curiosity, ambition and sensuality to the austere order of an ascetic Epicureanism.

He should have been born a Cardinal in fifteenth-century Florence, privy councillor to the Pope, special envoy to the palace of the Doge in Venice, spending his years drinking, loving, idling about the canals, writing, keeping his silence — and negotiating the most satanic, involved and scandalous affairs of the Catholic Church.

I discern his countenance in the dark, on the divan — at times his expression is Mephistophelian and ironic and his beautiful black eyes sparkle suddenly when a tiny flicker of light from the candle hits them. Then again he shifts, full of finesse, decline and weariness.

His voice is filled with affectations and color — and I am pleased that his sly, coquettish, painted, embellished, sinful old soul is expressed with such a voice.

Tonight as I see him and hear him for the first time, I understand how wise such a complicated, heavily burdened soul of sanctified degeneracy was in succeeding to find its form in Art — its perfect match — and be saved.

The casually impromptu but sagely studied verse of Cavafy, his deliberately inconsistent language, his unaffected rhyme, is the only body that could faithfully embrace and reveal his soul.

Body and soul are one in his poems. Seldom has such an organically perfect unity existed in the history of literature.

Cavafy is among the last remaining flowers of a civilization. With double, faded leaves, with a long, sickly stem, without seed.

Cavafy has all the typical characteristics of an exceptional man in an age of decline — wise, ironic, sensual, charming and brimming with memory. He lives *as if indifferent, as if courageous.* Reclining on a soft couch he gazes out of his window and waits for the *barbarians*[14] to appear. He holds a parchment with delicate, finely scriptured praises. He is dressed in his holiday finery, painted with care, and he waits. But the barbarians don't come, and toward nightfall he sighs softly and smiles ironically at the naïveté of his soul in hoping.

Tonight I look at him and rejoice at this courageous soul that passively, without strength and without discouragement, belatedly bids farewell to the Alexandria he is losing.

"Aren't you drinking at all! It's from Chios, I swear! Why have you become so quiet?"

He bends over and fills my glass and for a moment there is a glint of sarcasm and nobility in his eye.

But I kept silent because I was thinking of his magnificent poem, "God Forsakes Antony," and did not answer because I was repeating it slowly to myself:

When suddenly at the midnight hour
an invisible troupe is heard passing
with exquisite music, with shouts —
do not mourn in vain your fortune failing you now,
your works that have failed, the plans of your life
that have all turned out to be illusions.
As if long prepared for this, as if courageous,
bid her farewell, the Alexandria that is leaving.
Above all do not be fooled, do not tell yourself
it was only a dream, that your ears deceived you;
do not stoop to such vain hopes.
As if long prepared for this, as if courageous,
as it becomes you who are worthy of such a city;
approach the window with firm step,
and listen with emotion, but not
with the entreaties and complaints of the coward,
as a last enjoyment listen to the sounds,
the exquisite instruments of the mystical troupe,
and bid her farewell, the Alexandria you are losing.[15]

That same evening, a farewell banquet.

I shall never forget that evening because I believe it characterizes the critical era we live in. It is the threat that hangs in the air. Anxiety pierces even the most cordial, cherished hours and gives a warlike flavor to friendship.

There were about fifteen of us. We ate together, laughed for a while, and then a man, who was my junior, turned to me, with gloom and agitation:

"We must talk tonight before you leave. Much of what you have written in *Anagenesis*[16] we do not accept."

He held on to me and shuddered with love and aversion as he looked at me.

And I, who delight in the younger generation, with my ear forever cocked, alert, anxious and rapacious in their presence, was glad.

"We shall wrestle," I answered laughingly. "You will give your opinion and I will give mine — and let Charon take whom he may!"

We all sat around a big table, appointed Dr. Paul Petrides our chairman, and the wrestling began.

I knew we would not be talking about Art. A few years ago this superior intellectual circle of Alexandria would have sat up till dawn discussing Palamas and Cavafy and the problems of art and aesthetics, and would have recited verses. Now, for as many days as I was with them, we rarely spoke, even in passing, about scholars and literary works. The soul had shifted — the front line of battle had changed direction. All of this seemed old to us, vain adornments, occupations for idle and backward people.

And so, tonight, a polemic wind had settled around us. The younger men were pale, spoke sparingly and forcefully. They spoke as young men should — unhesitatingly. They were rigid, unyielding, without polyhedric tricks of the mind. They believed.

We spoke — with emotion, as though in confession — about contemporary man's obligation, our duty. Among all the various factions that are organized, in which should each of us enlist and how should each of us fight?

It wasn't long before this evening's friendly meeting was transformed into a council of war. As though we were truly in a state of siege and had gathered together to decide our course of action.

We divided into two major camps.

Some supported the notion that economic causes are always History's first motives. Only these can enlighten the evolution of life and guide our thought and action. All other motives are secondary and derivative.

Others disagreed. One, in expressing his thought said:

"I often doubt whether economic causes alone can explain everything. Only if I'm pressed do I accept this economic universal domination.

"If I'm pressed. In other words, if from theory I am forced to go to action. Whoever theoretically inspects the evolution of human activity may sometime find himself obliged also to accept the spiritual factor as the prevailing lever of History. However, whoever abandons theory and plunges into action is forced to accept only the economic factor in order to have firm ground upon which to walk and build. Otherwise he will lose himself in mystical, dangerous ambiguities."

When my turn came to give my opinion, too, I must confess I was somewhat moved. This was a friendly banquet; my friends were bidding me farewell, but the moment surrounding us is so critical that it does not tolerate sentimentalities. And my friends were looking at me with severity, and waited.

I tried, with a few words, to state my credo:

"I am a monist. I feel deeply that Matter and Spirit are one. Within me I feel only one essence.

"However, when I am forced to express myself as I am tonight, and formulate this essence, I am forced, naturally, to express myself with words, that is to say, with logic. Consequently, following the nature of logic, I am compelled to separate what by nature is inseparable. And since human senses are limited, out of all the infinite, probable aspects or sources, if you will, of reality, I distinguish only two: that which we call Matter and that which we call Spirit.

"One word only: Matter or Spirit, as I understand it, would express only part of the first essence, because each of these words has been reduced by usage to have one specific narrow content.

"That is why, when I want to formulate with words that which is one, I also separate in two even the highest motives of History — of the individual or the group: HUNGER and PATHOS.

"I use the word *pathos* and not the word *spirit* because this word has assumed an ideological, immaterial distilled content that is incomprehensible and hateful to me. 'Spirit' contains a great deal more 'matter' than materialists imagine; just as 'matter' contains a great deal more 'spirit' than idealists imagine.

"Therefore, I can state my thought roughly as follows: Hunger, the economic cause, is normally the first motive — that is, most of the time. But in critical times (anger, hatred, love, reproductive instinct, etc.) the first motive is pathos.

"However, according to what I said earlier, when we look deeper into our differences, we see them disappearing."

This is how we talked, and dawn was almost breaking.

SINAI

SINAI

For years Sinai, the God-trodden mountain, gleamed in my mind like an inaccessible summit. The Red Sea, Arabia Petraea, the little harbor of Raitho, the long camel caravan in the desert, the treacherous inhuman mountains over which the groaning Jews wandered for forty years, and finally, the holy monastery built upon the *burning but not consumed bush* — here was a goal I had been yearning to fulfill during all the years I was led astray in the big cities.

Galilee, with its idyllic charm, its serene harmonious mountains, its blue sea and tiny enchanting lake, spreads out behind the shoulders of Jesus, smiling, resembling him — the way a mother resembles her child. Galilee is a simple and shining commentary out of the text of the New Testament. Here God appears peaceful, temperate, cheerful, like a good man.

But it was the Old Testament that always stirred me, and related far more profoundly with my spirit. When I would read this raw, all-avenging thunderbolt of a Book, which smolders when you touch it, like the mountain upon which God descended, I would throb with longing to go and see with my own eyes, and touch the abominable mountains where it was born.

I shall never forget a short impetuous dialogue I once had in a garden with a woman.

"I'm disgusted with poetry, art and books," I said. "They all seem insipid to me, made of paper. It's as though you were hungry and instead of being given meat, bread and wine, you're given the menu, and you chew it like a goat."

I spoke angrily. The woman before me was pale, with broad cheekbones and a wide mouth like a Russian peasant.

"This is how our vapid souls satisfy their hunger today . . . like goats."

Laughing, she answered: "You speak to me with anger, and yet I'm in agreement with you. There's only one book — the Old Testament, because it isn't made of paper, but drips blood. It's all flesh and bones. To me the Bible is like chamomile tea for naïve and ailing people. Jesus was truly like a lamb, slaughtered on the green grass at Easter, unresisting, bleating lovingly. But Jehovah is my God. Hard, like a barbarian who emerges out of the dreaded wilderness with a hatchet in his belt. With this hatchet Jehovah opens my heart and enters."

In a little while the pale woman spoke more softly:

"Do you remember how he talks with the people? Have you seen how men and mountains are ground in the palms of his hands? Have you seen how kingdoms act at his feet? Man cries out, weeps, resists, hides under rocks, burrows underground. He struggles to elude him. But Jehovah is nailed to his loins like a knife."

Thus spoke the pale woman in the sun-drenched garden; and from that moment the longing ignited in me to go to the lair where the bloodthirsty God was born, and enter — as we enter the lion's den.

And this morning when I beheld Arabia Petraea, and the upright mountains beyond that were steaming under the sun, I trembled with joy and fear. I was entering the lion's den.

Raitho is the charming little port of Sinai. Its few houses are scattered along the edges of the seashore and red, yellow and black caïques splash in the green sea. Sweet serenity. The mountains are a light blue, the sea aromatic like watermelon. My companion, the painter Kalmouhos, turned to me laughing:

"We made a mistake, can't you see? We've come to a Greek island, we've come to Siphno!"

But in the distance you could see the palm trees, and two camels appeared on the mall. They turned their heads to the sea for a moment, shook themselves, and with two or three slow swaying strides, disappeared among the houses.

We walked, and our hearts danced as we trod the fine sand. Could all this simple quiet spectacle be a trick of our minds? The sand was full of huge seashells, the renowned seashells of the Red Sea. The houses were built of fossilized trees from the sea, of calcified coral and sponge, of sea stars and enormous shells. The people gleamed, almond-eyed and darkskinned, in their white flowing djellabas. A chocolate-colored little girl was playing on the white sandy beach, clad in a brilliant color of Bougainvillaea.

There were several European houses made of wood, with verandas and beautiful doll-like symmetrical gardens, and empty fruit cans strewn about the streets. Two Englishwomen were reading under a huge green parasol and their deathly whiteness made you gasp.

Beach after beach, we finally arrived at the Sinai dependency. From here we would take the camels and set out for the God-trodden mountain. There was a large courtyard, surrounded by the monks' cells, guesthouses, the two

Greek schools for boys and girls, storerooms, the oil press, kitchens — and in the center of the courtyard, the church.

And crowning all this was the biggest miracle in the wilderness: Archimandrite Theodosios, the abbot of Matohiou; the warm, all-loving heart of man.

Rarely do Greeks come to this wilderness. And Archimandrite Theodosios, tall, majestic, a fiery Greek from Tsesmes of Asia Minor, welcomed us as he would have welcomed Greece herself, with all the exquisite ritual of the priestly hospitality that I loved so well: the spoonful of sweet preserves, the cold water, the coffee, the well-laden table with the white fragrant tablecloth, the joy which lights up the faces of those who serve the guest . . .

Through the window the Red Sea sparkled. Opposite, etched in mist, the mountains of Thebes were drowned in light. I talked with the abbot about the *three score and ten palm trees* that the Scriptures say were found in this village of Raitho by the Hebrews after they crossed the Red Sea. Then I asked about the *twelve wells of water*. It was like asking about relatives upon returning to my country after a long absence. All these biblical questions were so beautifully harmonized to this vast wilderness surrounding us and the mountains opposite, where the great ascetics struggled. And when I learned that the palm tree orchard was still alive and the sources of water were still flowing, I rejoiced.

I have tasted such happiness often in my life — a glass of water at the end of a journey; a simple shelter, a human heart living unknown in some corner of the world, warm and unspent, awaiting the stranger. And when the stranger appears at the end of the road the heart leaps joyfully because it has found a human being. And as in love, so it is with hospitality, surely he who gives is more happy than he who receives.

The three camel drivers, Taema, Mansour and Aoua, who were to take us up to the peak of Sinai, arrived in their colorful djellabas. They were wearing three wreaths of camel's hair around their heads and each had a long yataghan that was slung over his shoulder by a strap. Resilient Bedouins, lean-legged, with round, eagle eyes, they greeted us touching their palms to their heart, lips and forehead.

Each was leading his camel, which was loaded in a towering heap with food, a tent, army cots and blankets for the journey. We were to remain in the desert three days and three nights.

We learned a few words — the most indispensable for our three-day sojourn with the Bedouins: fire, water, bread, God and salt.

The camels, their trappings adorned with orange and black furry tassels, kneeled, groaning with rancor, their beautiful eyes glistened without kindness, resentfully.

"Give the camels a few dates for their sweet tooth," ordered the abbot.

And Polycarpos, the fair Cypriot deacon, brought dates in a peasant's bag and divided them among the Bedouins and the camels.

We set out and almost instantly were plunged in the boundless desert. Abruptly, just a step from the monastery, the desert begins, gray, endless, barren.

The rhythm of the camel, undulating and patient, overtakes your body. The blood regulates itself rhythmically with this motion, and as the blood flows, so flows the soul of man. Time frees itself from the mathematical cubicles into which it has been squeezed by the rational Western mentality. Here, with the heaving of the "ship of the desert," time rediscovers its primordial rhythm, it becomes a flowing and indivisible essence, a light mystical vertigo that transubstantiates thought into reverie and music.

After hours of surrendering myself to this rhythm, I understood why the Anatolians read the Koran swaying back and forth, as though riding a camel. This is how they communicate to their soul the monotonous motion without end that will bring them to the great mystical desert — ecstasy.

We had been walking for five hours on this fair sand. By now the sun had set and we had finally reached the foot of the mountain. Taema, who was leading the way, halted and gave the signal to camp.

"*Krrr! Krrr!*" came from the depths of the guides' throats, and the panting camels laboriously kneeled forward, then abruptly fell back on their haunches, like houses collapsing.

We unloaded them and pitched our tent. Aoua ran and gathered some twigs and we lit a fire while Mansour took the pan, butter and rice from the straw basket and started the cooking.

The cold was biting. We sat around the fire and Kalmouhos set himself to drawing various animals on a piece of paper and asking:

"*Phi kaplan?*" (Are there lions?)

And the Bedouins, staring with surprised glee at the sketch of the lion, shouted:

"*Phi! Phi!*"

"*Phi taampin?*" (Are there snakes?)

"*Phi! Phi!*"

Taema, meanwhile, was stirring a frothy corn flour in water. With his swarthy, slender fingers he shaped it in the pan and began to bake it like unleavened bread. The pilaf soon emitted its aroma and we all sat down together and ate. We brewed tea, smoked, talked, and when the fire died down and we could no longer see, we fell silent.

A secret joy overtook my soul. I fought to stifle all this romanticism — the desert, Arabia, the tent, the Bedouins — and mockingly laughed at my heart for fluttering and pounding so.

As I stretched out in the tent and closed my eyes all the muffled, inscrutable murmuring of the desert spilled over my mind. The camels lying outside the tent were chewing their cud and I could hear their jaws slowly grinding away happily. All the desert was chewing its cud like a camel.

At dawn the next day we began our journey through the mountains — desolate, waterless, unfriendly mountains, that despise man and repel him. Occasionally an ashen wild partridge beat her wings with a metallic sound in the black craggy caves. Now and then a crow would fly over us in circles as though wanting to scent us out before deciding what to do.

All day long there was the rhythm of the camel, the monotonous lulling song of Taema, the sun that beat down on us like fire and the sizzling air over the rocks and our heads.

We were following the inhuman road that the Hebrews had taken three thousand years ago when they fled Egypt. This wilderness we now traversed served as the dreadful workshop in which the race of Israel had hungered, thirsted, hardened and been forged. I gazed with insatiable eyes at the cliffs one by one, following the winding road in the ravine, imprinting all these blazing mountain ranges in my mind. I remembered once on a Greek seashore I had walked for hours through a grotto filled with heavy stalactites and gigantic stone phalli, which glittered brilliantly crimson in the light of the torch. This grotto was the sheath of a large river that had now gone dry because the riverbed had changed course over the ages.

It suddenly flashed through my mind that this ravine beneath the sun we were now passing was exactly like that other. Jehovah, the pitiless God, had dug out these mountain ranges in order to pass through. Before he crossed this wilderness Jehovah had not yet firmly defined his image — because his people had not yet become firmly defined. The Elohim were scattered about in the air; they were not one but innumerable spirits, anonymous and invisible. The Elohim blew the spirit of life into the world, procreated, united with women, killed, descended upon the earth like lightning and thunder. They had no country and belonged to no land or tribe.

But little by little they took on flesh. They sought out huge rocks in elevated regions. The people smeared these rocks with oil, poured blood on them, and offered sacrifices. Whatever is most loved by man is what must be offered as sacrifice to God in order to win his good graces and so they offered him their firstborn son, the highest possession of man.

Slowly, through the centuries, with easy living, the race softened, became civilized; its God, too, softened and became civilized. They no longer slaughtered human sacrifices to him, but animals. He was no longer unapproachable and unseeable, but condescended to accept forms within the reach of the human eye: a golden calf, a winged sphinx, snake, hawk . . .

Thus the fearsome God of the Hebrews began to become diluted and lose himself in the rich serene land of Egypt. But suddenly the fierce Pharaoh intruders came, uprooted the Hebrews from the rich fields, and threw them far into this barren deadly Arabian desert. Now started the hunger and thirst, rage and rebellion. It must have been here where they stopped one afternoon, hungry and thirsty, and cried out: "Would to God we had died by the hand of the Lord in the land of Egypt, when we sat by the fleshpots and when we did eat bread to the full!" And Moses, despairingly, savagely, raised his arms to God and shouted: "What shall I do with this ungrateful people? They are ready to pick up stones and kill me!"

And God bent down over his people and listened. Sometimes he sent them quails and manna to eat, at other times the sword to cut them down. With each passing day here in the wilderness his face became more fierce, and every day he approached his people more closely — becoming fire at night and marching before them, and a column of smoke by day. He roosted in the Ark of the Covenant and the Levites would leave him on the ground, and not a soul dared approach him.

His face was constantly narrowing, getting harsher, taking on the appearance of Israel and becoming more firmly defined. He was no longer a mass of anonymous, homeless, invisible spirits spilled in the air; he was no longer the God of all the Earth. He had become Jehovah, the hard, avenging, bloodthirsty God of one race only, the race of the Hebrews — because he was going through difficult times, fighting with the Egyptians, the Amalekites, the Midianites and with the wilderness. Through suffering, scheming, killing, he had to conquer and save himself.

This treeless, waterless, inhuman ravine through which I was passing is the terrible sheath of Jehovah. Here is where he passed, roaring.

How can you know and feel the Hebrew race without crossing and living through the terrifying desert? We crossed it on camel for three interminable days. The throat gets parched from thirst, the temples reel, the mind whirls as it follows, snakelike, the winding, glistening ravine. How can a race that was forged in this furnace for forty years die? I, who love this unrelenting race, delighted in looking at the savage rugged rocks upon which its virtues were honed; the will, the perseverence, the stubbornness, the endurance and, above all, a God, flesh of their flesh, to whom they cried: "Give us food to eat! Kill our enemies! Give us the Promised Land!" And they compelled him by force to obey.

The Jews who continue to live and rule over the world through their virtues and vices are indebted to this wilderness. Today, in the transitory period of rage, vengeance and violence, the Jews are of necessity once again the chosen people of the formidable God of Exodus *from the land of bondage.*

Ah! How deeply I breathed this heroic primordial air!

How will we, today, be able to solidify the contemporary terrifying countenance of our God? How can we find the simple Word that will be able to encompass all of God's riches, the antinomies, his hatreds and loves, his joy and sorrow, his great strength and incurable weakness? The true God disdainfully passes over our human virtues, the daughters of fear. He is the God of destruction and at the same time of creation, death and love together. He procreates, impregnates and kills, and again he procreates, eternally dancing beyond the boundaries of logic, virtue and hope.

God is the dark unknown all-probable explosive power, that breaks out even in the smallest particle of matter.

I pass through this God-creating Arabian desert and all of man's contemporary agony pounds in my temples. How can we, too, be saved, creating the contemporary Savior, flesh of our flesh, the Hero who will lead us to the modern Promised Land?

Every Savior preaches the Word according to his race, the age in which he was born, and his individual makeup. But all Saviors are one. In word and in deed they always express the same prehuman, human and metahuman Cry. God agonizes within human bodies, he wrestles to utter one Word, to unburden himself, but he cannot; he only raves and groans. But suddenly, in one upward thrust of his whole dark multiheaded body, he gives birth to the Hero. What does this mean, "he gives birth to the Hero"? He becomes a Hero. And as soon as the inarticulate Cry rings clear, memory is illuminated, God acquires vision, and unstumblingly pushes forward on earth for a few centuries.

The Hero speaks and all creation rejoices because it recognizes its own voice. He acts and the entire universe rallies to his side and wants to follow him, as though sensing this is what it wanted, this is the action it wanted to take from the beginning of time.

The Hero, that is to say, the most perfect expression of God in an age and a race, gives cohesion and memory to the struggle, and this entire world is his gift to man. We see with his eyes, we hear only what he first heard, we eat the crumbs from his rich table, like dogs and like Lazaruses. We cannot pass where he has not opened the way and we cannot utter a word that he did not create. The rock is dry and barren before us, until he comes and strikes it and waters gush forth to refresh us all. Life has been reduced to a stagnant quagmire and he comes, the spirit of upheaval, and churns the waters and cures the paralytics.

Innumerable things sit in the shade of nonexistence and

wait for the Hero to give them a name, that is to say, life and worth. All hearts, even the most unworthy, involuntarily cry out: "Touch me so that I may burn and be saved with you."

Chaos takes on form. Man loses his fear and becomes gentler. He begins with confidence to work the soil and his mind again. He enlarges and broadens human destiny as much as he can.

The Hero is not an unexpected heavenly phenomenon. His roots are deep in the masses. And the most insignificant parent contributes unknowingly to the birth of the Hero. Without knowing it, every effort of the masses aims at this remote end: to create the Hero, the Messiah, and be saved.

The Jews believe that the Messiah will come if they perform good deeds; he will not come, he cannot come, even if he wanted to, if the Jews fall into indolence and unfaithfulness. Every good and generous action compels him to draw closer, every evil and cowardly act keeps him distant. Thus the Messiah is dependent on all human acts. He is created by man, by all men, the small and the great. And more profoundly: salvation comes not from the Messiah but from the act of every individual, separately, and from the race jointly.

But gradually, as time passed, the Jews were no longer able to endure this harsh teaching that imposed such responsibility on them. They wanted to see the coming of the Messiah in their short lifetime and to enjoy their reward and redemption in this life. So they invented minor Messiahs of their own stature: the Sabbath and the great Day of Atonement. All week they can commit injustices, be unfaithful and covetous, and all is forgiven because the Sabbath, the weekly Messiah, will come; if on this day they are pure and immersed in prayer, all the wrongs of the week are forgiven. In like manner they also await the yearly Messiah, the Day of Atonement, for all the sins of the year.

The Hero of any race always sets the Impossible as his goal; but quickly the masses invent little expediencies, convenient goals within easy reach, and are relieved.

But we should always set the Impossible as our goal. The masses will always find their way — that is, the adaptation of their need and strength to this inaccessible ideal. But the higher the ideal shines, the higher is the elevation of the masses and the closer the small convenient gods approach the awesome countenance of the Invisible.

Around noon today we were due to reach the Sinai Monastery. We had finally climbed to the Midian plateau, over fifteen hundred meters above sea level, after having spent the previous night in a Moslem cemetery, with our tent pitched beside a sheik's tomb.

We awakened at dawn in the stinging cold. Snow had covered our tent and the whole broad plateau lay before us stark white. Tearing the roof off a broken-down shack of the cemetery we started a fire. Joy! Flames licked the air and we all huddled around them to get warm. The camels came, too, and stretched their necks over us. We drank raki made from dates, and brewed tea, then the Bedouins spread a small straw mat on the snow, kneeled, and facing Mecca, began to pray.

Their innocent sunburned faces, plunged ecstatically in their simple primitive God, were radiant. With deep reverence I watched these three careworn, hungry bodies being gladdened and fulfilled. Mansour, Taema and Aoua had been transported into the heavens. I could feel the gates of paradise open for an instant and let them in. Their own paradise, the Moslem, Bedouin paradise: sun, young camels and ewes grazing in a green pasture, colorful camel's-hair tents, women chatting outside, painted with henna and kohl and two false beauty marks on their cheeks, silver bracelets around their ankles and arms; food is steaming, there's rice with milk, white bread, a handful of dates and a pitcher of cold water. Three of the tents are bigger than the others, three camels swifter than the others and three women more beautiful than the others — the tents, camels and women of Mansour, Taema and Aoua . . .

When, at the end of the prayer, paradise closed its gates and our three Bedouins descended to the Midian plateau and saw us sitting near the fire waiting, they came and sat beside us again without speaking, and patiently resumed their humble earthly tasks.

Kalmouhos, my companion, had gotten up and was playing with the snow, and I gently reached out my hand to Taema and spoke confidingly to him:

"La illah ilallah, Muhammadan rasoul, Allah!" ("There is only one God, and Mohammed is his Prophet.")

Taema was stunned. It was as though I had discovered his secret. He looked at me, beaming with joy, and squeezed my hand.

We set out. Kalmouhos and I went on foot as it was cold and we were impatient. We could no longer bear the indolent, patient rhythm of the camel.

The harsh mountains of green and red granite wondrously unfolded to our right and left. Now and then a graceful little bird would flit by, black, with a stark white head. Kalmouhos called it "jockey."

A line of camels appeared at the end of the road and for an instant gleamed against the red bosom of the mountain like a sculptured bas-relief. We paused for a while and the arriving Bedouins greeted us with their heartfelt greeting:

"*Salaam aleikum!*" ("Peace unto you!")

And when they reached the three guides we watched them clasp hands, bend over each other's shoulder, cheek to cheek, and speak to one another with hushed voices in a long drawn-out greeting.

This is the warmhearted meeting of men we saw during our three-day journey. When Bedouins meet in the desert each bends over the other, they clasp hands tightly, and the simple age-old stichomythia begins: "How are you? How is your wife? How is your camel? Where do you come from? Where are you going?" The one who is asked responds and when he finishes he, too, asks the same questions and then the response of the other begins. The words *salaam* and *Allah* are heard repeatedly and this encounter takes on the sacred lofty meaning that man's encounter with man should always have.

I look with emotion at these children of the desert, with their age-old traditions, with their simple, grasping souls. They live on a few dates, a handful of corn, a cup of coffee. Their bodies are worn and lean, their legs all sinew and slender like a goat's, their eyes and ears keen like an animal's.

Their lives have not changed in thousands of years. The leader of their race, the sheik in the red burnoose, judges them according to the unwritten Bedouin law. So religious is their respect for property that you can leave anything in the desert, carve a circle around it, and the area becomes inviolable.

Tents are their permanent dwelling places and the improvised little huts they build are not to be lived in but are used for storing all their humble wealth: flour, rice, coffee, sugar, tobacco. They can move to another location, leave their little houses open for months, and they always remain inviolable.

If you are passing a stranger's date grove and eat of his dates and leave the pits in a heap around the tree, the owner of the date grove is glad to have been a benefactor to a hungry wayfarer. If, however, he finds the pits scattered far from the tree, the owner is angered and pursues the thief and avenges himself savagely upon his camels and sheep.

They are the most impoverished and most hospitable people in the world. They will go hungry but will not eat in order always to have something in their tent to offer a stranger. They never beg, even though they are hungry. In Raitho I was told of a young Bedouin girl who was watching some tourists eating, and when they saw her and offered her something she refused, out of pride, and the next moment fainted and collapsed from hunger.

The Bedouin's great love is his camel. I watched how Taema's, Aoua's and Mansour's delicate ear lobes twitched uneasily when they heard the slightest gasp coming from one of the camels. They would stop, adjust the saddle, feel the camel's stomach, gather whatever dry grass they could find and feed it. And at night they would unsaddle it, cover it with a woolen cloth, spread a towel on the ground and, hunched over, would carefully remove the dirt from its fodder, bit by bit.

An old Arabic song uses bold similies to praise this beloved companion of the Bedouin:

The camel treads upon the sand and goes forward. She is as solid as the coffin's planks. Her thighs are firm and resemble a high fortress gate. The rope marks on

*her ribs are like dried-up lakes filled with pebbles. Her
skull is as hard as an anvil. Touch her and you think
you are touching a file. The camel is exactly like the
aqueduct that was built by the Greek master craftsman
who covered its peak with tiles.*

We had left the camels behind and were hurrying up the
mountain, trembling with anticipation at the prospect of
finally coming upon the monastery. We passed a small
water puddle, a few date trees, a stone hut. Farther down,
an iron cross was propped against a cliff. At last we were
approaching.

And suddenly, from the peak of a cliff, Kalmouhos'
joyful cry:

"Derr!" ("The monastery!")

Below us, on an open stretch of land between two towering mountains, the renowned Monastery of Sinai appeared
like a fortress surrounded by mulberry bushes. The purpose of our journey. I had so longed for this moment all my
life, and now that I held the fruits of my great labors in my
hands I rejoiced quietly, without speaking, and was in no
hurry.

For a second I felt an impulse to turn back. The harsh
joy flashed through me not to reap and enjoy this fruit of
my longing. But, alas, a gentle breeze blew, laden with the
scent of blossoming trees. Like almond trees. The summit
of my soul was conquered, the inner man who deigns to
accept joy and sweetness won, and I proceeded forward.
Kalmouhos was already running ahead, singing.

Now we could easily discern the monastery — the mulberry trees, the towers, the church, the cypress trees. In a
little while we reached the gardens. My heart leaped in
surprise and joy. I raised myself over the hedge and saw —

glistening in the sun, in the middle of the desert — olive trees, orange trees, walnut trees, fig trees and enormous blossoming almond trees. Sweet warmth, fragrance, the humming of tiny laboring insects.

For a long while I savored this smiling face of "God," who loves men and is made of earth, water and human sweat.

For three days now I had been confronting the other face, the frightful, unblooming, all-granite one. I had thought to myself: this is the true God, the fire that burns, the granite that is not carved out of human desires. And now, leaning over the hedge into this flowering orchard, I live the words of the ascetic: *God is a quiver and a gentle tear.*

"There are two kinds of miracles," says Buddha, "those of the body and those of the soul. I do not believe in the first; I believe in the second." The Monastery of Sinai is a miracle of the soul. For fourteen centuries now this monastery that was built around a well of water in the fiercest desert, in the midst of rapacious tribes of hostile religions and other tongues, rises like a fortress and resists the natural and human forces that besiege it.

After a three-day journey through the unsmiling desert, the moment I beheld the monastic blossoming almond trees, my heart leaped. I sensed that here a superior human conscience existed; that here human virtue conquers the desert . . .

I stroll through the date groves of the monastery becoming oriented. Here I am, in the midst of the biblical mountains, on the lofty landscape of the Old Testament. Towering before me to the east is the Mountain of Knowledge, where Moses nailed the serpent of brass. The land of the Amalekites and the Amorite Mountains are just beyond.

The desert of Kedar, Idumaea and the Tahiman Mountains stretch northward all the way to the Moab Desert. To the south lies Cape Pharan and the Red Sea. Finally, toward the west, the mountain range of Sinai, the "Holy Summit" where God spoke to Moses, and a short distance away, Saint Catherine's.

Between the mountains, at a height of fifteen hundred meters, the Monastery of Sinai is built like a quadrangle fortress, with towers and embrasures. I look down upon its grand courtyard. The church gleams in the center, with a little white mosque beside it; the crescent here joins in brotherly fashion with the cross. All around, sparkling white, are the snow-covered monks' cells, storerooms and guesthouses.

Three monks are sitting in the sun warming themselves, their words reverberating clearly in the profound morning stillness. One of the monks is telling of the wonders he saw in America — ships, bridges, cities, factories; the other is describing how they roast lamb on a spit in his country at Lidoriki; and the third is recounting the miracles of Saint Catherine — how the angels took her from Alexandria and carried her to the peak of Saint Catherine's and how the imprint of her body is still preserved on the cliff where they placed her.

The garden of the monastery sparkles in the snow and sun. The olive trees rustle quietly, the oranges glisten in their dark foliage, the cypress trees rise up ascetically in jet-black array. And permeating all this is an eerie sensation: slow, rhythmically, like someone breathing, the fragrance of the flowering almond trees comes and stirs your nostrils — your nostrils and your reason.

I wondered how this monastic citadel was able to resist these tranquil spring winds all these centuries and not fall, one spring. For years the expression uttered by the hardened hermit, Saint Anthony, has been agitating my heart with its deep human pain: "If you remain in the desert and your heart is tranquil and suddenly you hear the voice of a sparrow, your heart no longer can have its former serenity."

A pale fledgling monk climbed up to the tower where I was standing. He was an eighteen-year-old Cretan. We talked. Two blue shadows circled his eyes, and the thick down on his cheeks glistened as the sun struck it. Soon a sweet, gentle old man, about eighty, came up from the hatchway, panting heavily. He was worn out and no longer had the strength to desire either what was good or what was evil. His bowels were like Buddha would have wanted them — emptied.

The three of us sat on a bench in the sun and the young man took out a handful of dates from inside his shirt and offered them to us. The old man, rubbing his palm on his knee, began to tell me how the monastery was built and how it had struggled these many centuries. As I was sitting thus in the sun, surrounded by these unbelievable mountains, the legend of the monastery seemed to me like a simple and true fable:

"Around the well where the daughters of Jethro came to water their sheep and on the very spot where the *burning but not consumed bush* grew, Justinian built the monastery. At the same time the emperor sent out two hundred families from Pontus and Egypt to settle near the monastery, and become its guards and slaves.

"A century later Mohammed came into the world. He passed through Mount Sinai. The footprint of his camel is still preserved on a slab of red granite. He entered the monastery, and the monks welcomed him with great honors, and Mohammed was pleased and gave them the renowned testament, the *Achtiname*. It is still preserved, written in Kufic letters on roebuck leather and sealed with the palm of the Prophet.

"In this testament Mohammed grants generous privileges to the monks of Sinai: 'Should a monk of Sinai take refuge in a mountain or plain or cave or gorge or desert or house of worship, there I shall be with him and shall protect him from all harm. I shall defend them wherever they are, on land or on sea, east or west, north or south. All those who devoted themselves to the worship of God in the mountains and blessed places shall not be obligated to pay taxes or a tenth of the harvest, nor serve in the armed forces, nor pay fines. They shall be left in peace, because the wing of mercy spreads over them.'

"For centuries the monastery suffered hardships. The slaves that Justinian had sent became Moslems and they used torture on the monks in order to exact food and money from them. In fear the large gate was always kept closed and the fathers communicated through an underground passage that connected with the garden. The low iron doors and dark underground corridors are still preserved and there is a huge seven-fathom-high opening called a *touvara* through which the men and materials were hauled up by pulley.

"Now the heroic years are gone. The slaves have been tamed somewhat, the Bedouins have ceased their raids and the great gate remains open, without fear."

I shivered as I listened to this old man's remote voice, a voice not of this world, bringing the Byzantine walls to life all around me and filling the air with saints and martyrs. The ecstatic Cretan youth beside me was listening with gaping mouth to this wondrous legend. In the courtyard below, the monks were still carrying on their small talk quietly. Others in the cellar were inspecting and weighing the corn that the Arabs had brought. For a brief moment the door of the kitchen opened and I caught a glimpse of a huge table shimmering under the load of enormous lobsters that had been delivered the night before from the Aqaba Sea. Father Pahomios, the artist, was sitting on his threshold, wrapped in a blanket, painting a huge seashell.

I got up and walked down to the large terrace. The fathers were playing with the snow, making snowballs and frolicking like children. They were joyful that it had snowed and the desert would grow grass and the sheep and goats would eat and men would survive.

Men and women, descendants of the old slaves, had arrived and were huddled at the foot of the monastery. The men were smoking and talking loudly with grand gestures. The women, barefoot and dirty, covered with black maylahyas, wore their hair in a pointed bun like a saddle hook on their forehead. As they arrived, each of them quickly opened her maylahya and took out an infant and placed it on the rocks. Swarms of children had gathered and were holding out their hands, waiting for the *touvara* to open so their daily ration would be thrown down to them; three small loaves for each man and two for each woman or child. They had to come in person to receive this and each day they would set out from their huts, hours earlier, and come, in scorching heat or in snow. This is how they live. They also gather locusts and dry them and grind them to make bread.

The archbishop, the abbot of the monastery and *Archon of the Desert*, was leaning over the wall and laughingly tossing some colorful caps, which he had been saving for gifts, down to the children. And the Arab youngsters were howling with glee as they grabbed the unexpected gift that fell upon them from above, and soon their hard chocolate heads were gleaming yellow, red or green, each with a tassel stuck on top.

I watch these distant brothers with deep emotion. For centuries now they prowl about these Byzantine confines and the monks drop the small all-bran loaves of bread to them like stones. They live and die serving and threatening the monastery.

The monks recount their primitive traditions to me. Nothing has changed in thousands of years. They live as they did in the age of Jethro, the father-in-law of Moses; they marry and die; and just as they did then, only girls tend the sheep, and no one molests them. When two young people fall in love they steal away secretly at night and go up to the mountain. The young man plays the flute and the young woman sings, and they never touch each other. When the young man wants to ask for her hand in marriage, he goes to the tent of his father-in-law, sits outside and waits for the young girl to return from tending the sheep. As soon as she appears the young man jumps up and throws his burnoose over her and covers her.

When the time comes for the marriage pact to be sealed and for the groom to purchase the bride, the two fathers-in-law take a date leaf, pull it apart and divide it between them. Then the father of the bride says:

"I want a thousand pounds for my daughter."

Usually the groom doesn't have even one pound, but the Bedouins are proud and always follow this gracious formality of the marriage ritual.

As soon as the father-in-law mentions the thousand pounds, the sheik rises to his feet and says:

"Your daughter is worth two thousand pounds and the

105

groom wants to give this amount but as a favor to me, please waive five hundred."

And the father-in-law replies: "As a favor to our sheik, I waive the five hundred!"

Then the other relatives rise:

"Waive another hundred as a favor to me! And another hundred! And another fifty! And another twenty! . . ."

Until the amount has been reduced to one pound. At that moment the women who are grinding corn inside the tent cry out:

"Lou-lou-lou-lou!"

Then the father-in-law gets up and says:

"Oh, well, as a favor to the women who are grinding corn, I give my daughter for half a pound!"

The agreement is sealed; they eat, drink, squander whatever they have that first night; and then begins the dreadful daily life of the desert.

By now it was noon and we went down to the refectory, an arched medieval room with Gothic letters carved on the stone walls which the Latins, who lived with our people on Sinai for many years, must have built. Father Pahomios had painted the walls with fervent, childlike simplicity. A marvelous old fresco had been preserved at one end of the room depicting the Second Coming. Below it were three angels representing the Holy Trinity and standing between the wings of the three angels was the divine, God-descended pair, man and woman.

We sat down at the long table and the food was brought in — lobsters, greens, bread and a little wine. The fathers, about twenty of them, began to eat. No one spoke. The reader stepped up to the pulpit and began to read the in-

terpretation of the day's gospel: "The Return of the Prodigal."

For months on end I had experienced this rhythm at the
many monasteries I visited, where the meal takes on the
great mystical value that belongs to it. "When a virtuous
man is eating," a rabbi once said, "he liberates the God
who is in the food!"

In nasal tones the reader chanted on about the prodigal
son's sufferings; how he was forced to eat husks and
grieved; how one day he could no longer bear it and returned to his father — and from that day never budged
from his rich, noble, paternal home.

And I, in the midst of this Christian atmosphere of devout penitence, was thinking:

If only there were another monastery as I would like it,
in more perfect accord with the modern uplifting of our
soul, I would request them to read the excellent supple-
ment that one of our contemporaries added to the parable
of the prodigal:

The prodigal returned to his paternal home, weary, defeated and despairing. And at night when he stretched out
on his soft bed to sleep, the door opened quietly and his
younger brother entered.

"I want to leave! Our father's house can no longer hold
me!"

And the brother who had just this evening returned
defeated, rejoiced and embraced his brother and began to
counsel him: "This is what happened to me, but here is
how you must act; I was defeated, but you must hold
strong. Don't shame yourself as I did. Don't ever return
to this house!"

He bade him farewell, walked with him to the door and

cried with joy: "Perhaps he will turn out to be stronger than I was and not turn back."

Thus, Lucifer-like, while I was quietly eating with the fathers, smiling and listening to the parable, the prodigal was becoming transformed inside me, and the monastery that was befriending me was shaking at its foundations . . .

Dinner was finished. The fathers sat out in the sun while we, together with the archbishop, the sacristan and the prior went into the church.

One is stunned by the wealth — the air teems with silver candlesticks, the *iconostasis*[17] rises in golden splendor, the walls and columns shimmer with innumerable priceless icons.

Opening the huge reliquary, the sacristan heaped the sacred treasures of the monastery before us — holy relics, gold vestments, embroideries of superb Byzantine artistry profusely covered with pearls, miters glittering with precious stones, ivory carvings, valuable crosses, amulets, staffs . . .

All this gold and pearl treasure stored away in the desert for so many centuries!

And even more miraculous was the church, filled with the most exquisite Byzantine icons that I had ever beheld in my life — the most unique museum of hagiography in the world. In the altar apse there is a huge mosaic of the Transfiguration of Christ. To the left and right, Moses is shown as he is speaking with God and receiving the tablets with the commandments. Below are the twelve Apostles and the seventeen Prophets and in the corners, Justinian and Theodora.

The sacristan lit the candles and began to pray, and with religious awe he opened the large bier where the body of Saint Catherine reposed. Her hand was covered with rings and the royal crown adorned her head. Deeply moved, the devout Kalmouhos took his ring from his finger and offered it to the saint.

We reached the chapel of the Holy Bush and entered like Moses, barefoot. *Put off thy shoes from off thy feet, for the place whereon thou standest is holy ground.*[18]

The tiles are covered with valuable rugs. A brilliant mosaic of the Annunciation fills the niche of the altar. The chapel is dedicated to the Annunciation because the *burning but not consumed bush*[19] symbolizes the Virgin who received God in her body.

Beneath the Altar Table is the marble slab that covers the exact spot where the Holy Bush glowed before the eyes of Moses. *On a day when Moses was keeping the flock on the mountain he saw down near the water that there was a bush burning. Except that the fire was as a spring of water, so it kept the bush verdant with leaves and young shoots.*

We entered the library. It is famous for its manuscripts — Greek, Arabic, Kufic, Syrian. For a long while I savored the old books, the multicolored miniatures, the unfathomable mysterious manuscripts. Who knows, perhaps some Greek work of Sophocles, Sappho, Aeschylus that has been lost in the original may be preserved here in some Arabic translation.

I talked with Archbishop Porfyrion III. A saintly man, serene and learned. He lives at the monastery with the fathers and is struggling to bring back as much of the monastery's old grandeur as is possible.

With fervor and emotion he revealed his plans of reform to me.

"What we principally lack here at the monastery are young educated priests. We have bountiful treasures in our library and cannot take advantage of them. Foreigners want to publish these works but we're holding onto our treasures hoping soon to be able to publish them through our own Greek, our own Sinaitic enlightenment.

"We send young men to study for this specific purpose. We're going to set up our own printing shop and publish a periodical of our own. We plan to invite Greeks who possess special talents and provide them with the conveniences that will enable them to live here comfortably and work.

"We're going to do everything we can, with modern means, to complete the sacred mission of the Monastery of Sinai. Until now, we have preserved the treasures that you see in this library. In spite of the dangers, we have successfully completed the first part of our mission — the preservation of these works. Now begins the second — the publication.

"We are appealing to all Greeks: Let as many men of letters come here to help us. We will give them all our facilities and they will gain honor through researching and publishing our manuscripts.

"Let the Greeks know that an acropolis of Hellenism exists here, that for fourteen centuries has stood erect in the desert. Let them come and see us.

"Look at the guest book. In twenty-eight years, from 1897 to 1925, only thirty-five Greek tourists came. Look at how many foreigners came from the ends of the world: a hundred and forty-five English, sixty-nine French, fifty-eight Americans, sixty Germans — and how many Greeks? Only thirty-five. Thirty-five Greeks in twenty-eight years!"

The serene eyes of the archbishop kindled with emotion as he envisioned this hallowed ground of the monastery teeming with Greeks, working in the still solitude of the desert — like Benedictine monks.

110

I did not speak. I was uneasy. The Monastery of Sinai is in danger. Since the war, young men no longer come here who are learned and useful and can give it support. It, too, will be swept away by the descending squall.

This entire day had filled my heart with trepidation. The gold vestments, the pearls, the multicolored saints, the prodigal son, all merged in a monstrous reconstruction in the crucible of sleep.

And during the night, toward daybreak, at the hour when the bell tolled, I saw this ungodly dream:

The monastery seemed to be swarming with gypsies. They had entered the church with their clarinets and tambourines, their dogs and their sieves, and had set up camp. They had stretched a rope from the iconostasis to the vestibule and hung their red and yellow blankets and wet dresses.

The austere faces of the ascetics grew fierce, and long waving parchments with red letters unfolded from their mouths: *He who is victorious over nature rises above nature.* Saint Athanasios was there preaching: *Expect to be tempted for through temptation and wrongs suffered we enter the kingdom of heaven.* And from Saint Martinianos came the words: *Go forth brother to the desert and be saved.* Thorotheos, looking down from one of the columns, was preaching: *Brother, overcome the flesh.*

And the gypsies had hung a tambourine with red ribbons on the icon of the Virgin and had flung a yellow petticoat with black trim on the *Epitaphion.*[20] An old cross-eyed hag was at the bishop's throne teaching three young gypsy girls how to read fortunes. Young men were beating the drums and dancing, and an old man was playing the violin in a wild frenzy of joy. Suddenly everything vanished and

111

only a monkey remained to fill the vast darkness. It sat, squatting, with a little red cap, quietly removing the seeds of a rotted pomegranate . . .

We climbed the Holy Summit, the steep fortress where Moses saw God *face to face* and spoke with him. From a distance the jagged crest of the mountain looked like the mane of a wild boar.

The prophet says: "Ἵνα τί ὑπολαμβάνετε ὅρη τετυρωμένα; Τὸ ὅρος ὃ ηὐδόκησεν ὁ Θεὸς κατοικεῖν ἐν αὐτῷ—, which can be translated to mean: "Why do you take into account other mountains rich with vegetation, flocks and cheeses? There is only one true mountain, Sinai, to which God descended and dwells!"

Jehovah, the formidable Sheik of Israel, sits at the top of this Olympus of the Hebrews. He sits on its crest like fire and the mountain smolders. "Don't anyone touch it! Whatever touches Mount Sinai, whether man or beast, shall die! Whoever sees the face of God shall die!" As Athanasios says, "God is *Divine fire consuming.* Moses is *the pincers carrying God's burning coal.*"

Jehovah is this fire. In the desert innumerable spirits, the Elohim, who surveyed and governed all the world, were centralized in one fierce, jealous tribal God, protector of one race only — the Hebrew race. He is identified with fire. Whatever they threw into the fire for him to devour Jehovah devoured. They gave to Jehovah, that is, to the fire, their firstborn children — sons and daughters.

We climbed the thirty-one hundred steps which lead from the foot of the mountain to the Holy Summit, Father Pahomios following behind me with Kalmouhos. The two artists were in conversation. The simple, warmhearted hermit was leaning close, listening to the other artist who had come from the great world outside, bringing important news: how they mix colors today, how oils are made to dry faster, which are the best crayons.

We passed a small arched door opening on the cliffs. In the days when men trembled at touching the summit a confessor sat here and heard their confessions. "Whoever ascends the mountain of the Lord must have guiltless hands and a pure heart," commands David. "Otherwise he shall be killed." Today the door is deserted, the confessor has died, the summit no longer has the power to kill . . .

A little higher up we passed the cave where Elias saw his great vision: He entered the cave and, lo, there was the voice of God: "Go forth tomorrow and stand before the Lord on the mountain. And a strong wind will pass over you and shatter the mountain and crush the rocks; but the Lord will not be in the wind. After the wind there will be an earthquake; but the Lord will not be in the earthquake. And then, a fire; but the Lord will not be in the fire. And after the fire a sweet gentle breeze will blow; there is where the Lord will be!"

This is how the spirit always comes; after the gale, earthquake and fire, the sweet gentle breeze. And so it will come in our time. We are now passing through the earthquake period.

Farther up, Pahomios stopped and pointed out a crag to us:

"Here is where Moses stood on the day the Hebrews fought the Amalekites. As long as he held his arms up high, the Jews were victorious but when he grew tired and lowered them the Hebrews were put to flight. Then two priests, Aaron and Or, raised his arms and held them high until all the enemy had passed through the edge of the sword."

113

This entire mountain was covered with the superhuman tracks of the giant.

In Pahomios' guileless soul all these legends assumed a serene historical sense and he talked about them as though he were talking about gigantic antediluvian beings, dinosaurs and monsters, without a sign of trepidation or doubt in him.

When we reached the summit my heart bounded. Never had my eyes enjoyed such a sight. All of Arabia Petraea was before us with its dusky deep blue mountains. Beyond were the azure rocky mountain ranges of Arabia Felix and the green sea, sparkling like a turquoise. To the west the stark white desert, steaming in the sun, and beyond in the distance, the mountains of Africa.

An exotic landscape without water, without trees, without clouds; desolate. Like a landscape on the moon.

Here the soul of a despairing or proud man finds the ultimate bliss.

We entered the chapel on the peak. Father Pahomios was scratching the earth with his nails, trying to find traces of the old walls of the Byzantine church. He was pointing triumphantly to the stones carved into arches, the tiny Byzantine window columns, crosses, letters, ancient cisterns; searching furiously. Suddenly he gave out a great shout. He had discovered two Byzantine doves, with joined beaks, on a piece of marble — symbols of the Holy Spirit. It annoyed me to watch this innocent soul in his obsession with the doleful mania of finding and suspending and immobilizing life wherever he could, refusing to let the past go. Up here on this peak, where God is an elusive, wavering devouring flame, I found this spirit of excavation and preservation loathsome.

I turned to him and said:

"Father Pahomios, how do you imagine God to be?"

Pahomios looked at me, startled. He thought for a while and then said:

"Like a Father who loves his children."

"Aren't you ashamed?" I cried. "You dare speak that way about God on Mount Sinai? *God is consuming fire!*"

"Why do you tell me this?"

"So that you will abandon all these ruins and let Him burn them. Don't lift your hands against God, Pahomios!"

He shuddered and sat down, embarrassed. We opened the straw basket with the food and drank the wine and ate the bread, meat and oranges. I was carrying a small edition of Homer with me and began to read aloud the long idolatrous hexameters as though wanting to spite the Lord. The seacoasts of Greece spread out before me, the Gods of Olympus gleamed, the goddesses, all flesh, descended laughingly and united with the earthly men, and from this union gave birth, not to monsters and demons, but to heroes.

My heart steadied. Here in the smoke-blackened andirons of the Semetic god, the isolated heart awakens and grows brave. All the sins, the infractions and wretchedness of man are insignificant trifles in the face of his formidable struggle!

If the quibbling God of the Hebrews criticized man for his minor trespasses in the other life, how proudly man could exalt his defense!

"Yes, I sinned. I stole the wife and cow of my neighbor because they appealed to me; I killed my enemy because he wanted to kill me; with these hands I made idols and worshiped them! I lied because I was afraid; I hated my father because he stood in my way and would not let me pass! I broke all your commandments.

115

"But I tamed the earth, fire, water and wind. If I were not here the wild beasts and worms would devour you. You would rot in the mire from idleness and fear. I was the one who, in the midst of the blood and mud, cried out and asked for freedom. I, crying, laughing, stumbling, propped you up so you would not fall!"

These were the kind of things I imagined that day on Sinai's peak — the Apologia of man. Such was the dialogue between God and man.

But Pahomios was uneasy. It was getting dark and he was cold and came and roused me from the rock I was sitting on and we began our descent.

We took another path through a ravine covered with snow. Suddenly, the Arab who was walking ahead of us carrying the basket of food crouched over the snow.

"*Kaplan!*" he shouted joyfully.

We ran to see. Heavy imprints of a wild beast stood out in the snow.

"A lion!" cried Pahomios through distorted jaws.

Kalmouhos was jumping with joy, but the Arab explained that lions are frightened of humans and leave as soon as they catch their scent. Pahomios recovered. Kalmouhos' heart sank at missing such an opportunity.

I walked ahead, following the imprints of the beast, and was glad; in my mind Jehovah had passed over the snow and disappeared in terror into the desert.

Now the entire mountain is permeated with the presence, not of Moses any longer, but with that of a simple working man whom I loved dearly in my lifetime, George Zorba. For me, he is the one who now descends from Sinai, carrying the new Decalogue.

Zorba is an old mine worker, a great intrepid spirit, a

mind that is all lightning flashes and chasms. For months
the two of us lived together through many difficult times.
He is away now and does not write regularly because he
cannot hold a pen properly; he holds it like a chisel and
rips through the paper.

Once he wrote me these words and I carry them with
me at this moment, as I descend Mount Sinai, etched deep
in the tablets of my mind:

"According to my laws I do not fear God. I do not fear
death because it is nothing, just as I am nothing. I do not
fear the greatest elements of nature — cataclysms, earth-
quakes, illnesses, women. Whatever they may do, I laugh.
I say: Zorba, George Zorba, you are Nature's greatest element.

"I'm a Sinbad the Sailor. Not that I traveled to many
places, but I have robbed, killed, lied, cursed and slept with
plenty of women. I've broken all the commandments. How
many are there? Ten? Why shouldn't there be twenty, fifty,
a hundred, so I could break them all? And yet, if there is a
God, I will have no fear whatsoever to appear before him.
Because (I don't know how to tell you, so that you will
understand) all these things don't seem to me to have any
significance.

"There's a saying that God does not ask you what you
have eaten. And I say, neither does he ask you what you
have done. If I had two sons and the one was well behaved,
a homebody, thrifty, just and God-fearing, and the other
was roguish, iniquitous, a woman chaser, a fugitive — I
would certainly include them both at my table. I cannot
be sure, though, that my heart would not be closer to the
second. Perhaps, of course, because he probably resembles
me. But who is to say that I do not resemble God more

than our priest who does obeisances night and day and collects dimes?

"God indulges in revelry, he kills, perpetrates injustices, he loves, works, chases, just as I do. He eats what he likes, takes any woman he wants. You see a beautiful woman walking the earth like cool spring waters and your heart rejoices. And abruptly, the earth opens and she disappears. Where does she go? Who takes her? If she is virtuous we say, 'God took her.' If she is amorous, we say, 'the Devil took her.'

"But I believe that God and the Devil are one!"

We are in the company of Father Moses today, at the Chapel of Saint Catherine, perched 2,646 meters above the sea, on the highest peak of the Sinaitic mountain range.

The sun is dazzling and down below Arabia Petraea is steaming as far as the eye can reach.

Father Moses, a slender, short supple *Karpenisiotian*,[21] is sovereign here. He built the road that leads to the top of the mountain, strengthened the foundations of this tiny chapel upon whose terrace we are sitting, and now looks after the little guesthouse, which he has furnished with bedding, coal, food, icons and raki.

Our food is boiling. The two partridges we killed on the road are roasting on the embers and our likable Bedouin, Ferrangi, bends over them and pokes the fire. His strong lean body moves nimbly, full of youthfulness. Pahomios, wrapped in a blanket, is leaning over Kalmouhos' shoulder staring eagerly at the outlines of some mountains Kalmouhos is etching on a piece of paper.

The aroma of roasting partridges begins to fill the air and we huddle against the wall and wait; cold, hungry, and full of great joy.

Moses brings out some sweets, tea and raki made of dates. Then some walnuts, almonds and honey. And finally, a sweet black grape nectar that he had been storing since last year.

Moses delights in having guests to serve. He flutters about, comes and goes in the church, loosens the ropes on a pole that he had nailed on the highest rock and raises the Greek flag. He takes down the double-barreled shotgun and fires, then breaks into a *Klephtic*[22] Karpenisiotic song.

A good man, I reflected, can sanctify a place even over a distance of many kilometers. Here is this lean, humble monk who built a house on a steep, rugged peak, made a hearth, lit a fire and raised a flag. He overcame all the powers of evil. He overcame solemnity and sorrow and laughs and sings like a shepherd and his heart throbs because he has two unknown men before him to serve.

"How did you become a monk, Father Moses?"

And Father Moses jovially laughs ironically at himself and answers:

"I wanted to become a monk since I was twelve years old but the Devil kept presenting obstacles. And what obstacles you may ask. I'll tell you. My work was going well and I was making money. What does it mean 'to make money'? It means 'to forget God'!

"I was a postman, a vendor, a shoemaker, I worked in the mines of Lavriou and later I went to the railroads at Ikonio. I thought to myself, 'As soon as I lose my money I will go and become a monk.' God loved me. I cut the cord and left, just the way the cord of a balloon is cut and the balloon rises to the sky — that's how I left the world!

"I've been here twenty years now. What do I do? What I did in the world. I work. From morning to night I work.

119

You may well say, it's all the same, but I tell you, not at all! I'm happy here, but there, in the world, I wasn't.

"And how do I work? I build roads. All the roads we passed are mine. I build roads. This is my deaconship. This is why I was born. If I go to paradise I will go through the roads I build."

And he laughed, mocking his hopes:

"Pf! Paradise! Is that how one enters Paradise?"

Simple, well-fed Pahomios tightened his blanket about him, shivering, and murmured soothingly:

"You will enter, Moses . . . You will enter, Moses . . . don't worry."

Moses laughed:

"What do you have to fear? You hold a little brush and some colors and you paint paradise and enter.

"But as for me, it's an endless road. I have to build a road up to the very gates of paradise, otherwise I don't get in. Everyone according to his own works. And you," turning to Kalmouhos, "you will paint a wall, draw some trees, add waters and a few angels and you, too, will enter. Just like Pahomios. But what about you?"

He turned with great curiosity to me.

"I've already entered," I answered.

"For me paradise is a high mountain with a stone terrace on top. And on the terrace are walnuts, grapes, dates and raki, and I'm sitting with three good men and we talk about paradise!"

Thus talking, eating, drinking, carving our names into the rocks, the day passed. Bitter cold began to overtake us and we went into the little church.

The cliff upon which the angels had placed the body of Saint Catherine two hundred years ago had swelled and risen like bread and taken the shape of the reposing saint.

Moses was holding a lighted candle and was showing us the outline on the cliff of the saint's head, bosom and legs. He described her life and martyrdom to us, quietly, joyfully, simply — as though he were speaking of the earth: how it rained, how the harvest grew, how it was reaped . . .

We entered the monk's cell; lit the brazier. The muffled sound of thunder could be heard coming from a great distance.

Suddenly Kalmouhos, deeply moved by this blissful serenity turned to Moses:

"I'm going to paint you an icon of Saint Catherine, Father Moses, as a gift."

Moses coughed slyly.

"Why do you cough?"

"Hm, I wonder. I've heard that whoever paints an icon must first wash his hands thoroughly and must refrain from eating meat — do you understand me — and must not smoke. Only then will the icon perform miracles and be a thing of beauty."

The discussion was getting heated. Pahomios perked up his ears and listened.

Young, virile Kalmouhos — at the beginning of his art career — had grasped the mature white-bearded artist and was lecturing him:

"The artist must constantly have in his mind the life of the saint whom he wants to paint. He cannot think of anything else, day and night. And when should he take up his brush to paint? When he finally sees the saint in his dream."

Moses jumped up excitedly, deeply moved:

"Now I'm going to tell you something that until now I have never confessed to anyone. We said that my mission is to build roads. I torment myself all day. . . . In what

121

direction shall I take the road, to the right, left, where shall I build the bridge, where shall I open the ditch for the waters? I'm tortured with indecision. And at night I see in a dream where to build the road. That is why the roads are solid."

By now it was midnight and Ferrangi arrived loaded down with heavy blankets, which he spread out for us, and we went to sleep. At dawn, thick hail began to fall. We opened the tiny door and peered out at the dense impenetrable mist. It was bitter cold, and snow had completely covered the mountain.

"Put the kettle on to boil the tea!" ordered Moses as he closed the door.

Out came the brazier again and we prepared the tea. We began to chant psalms, our spirits rose, our blood warmed, and we decided to make our exit.

"Cross yourselves and pray, my good fellows," shouted Pahomios, shivering with cold and dread.

"There's no danger from the cold," retorted Kalmouhos, to frighten him, "but from the hungry beasts that roam about in this weather. Especially the bears!"

Pahomios crossed himself, went in and paid his respects to Saint Catherine, picked up a blanket, wrapped it around himself and followed the procession.

The snow was up to our knees; the hail resounded on our caps; laughing, cavorting, Moses in the lead, we followed the path he opened for us with his high boots.

We were returning to the monastery joyously, impatiently, as though returning to our paternal home.

At night, alone in my cell, I was leafing through the Old Testament, still harboring the vision of the desert deeply in my mind. The Bible seemed to me like a multipeaked mountain range from which the roaring prophets, tied with ropes, were descending. Rage erupts in the heart of the man who resists and struggles and is whirled about in the hands of God.

I suddenly grabbed some paper and began writing to unburden my heart:

"Samuel!"

The old prophet in the leather girdle and mottled rags was looking down at the city and didn't hear the cry of the Lord. The sun was a spur above the horizon in the sky and down below, sinful Gilgal was buzzing, wedged between the red rocks of Carmel with its swordlike palm trees and ripe thorny wild figs.

"Samuel," the voice of God cried out again: "Samuel, my faithful servant, you've grown old, can't you hear me?"

Samuel shuddered; his thick brows joined with rage, his long forked beard bristled wildly, and his ears echoed like shells of the sea. The curse neighed in his entrails like an unbridled mare.

"Anathema," he groaned, stretching his skeletal arm over his laughing, singing city that was buzzing like a wasp's nest; "Anathema to those who laugh, to the lawless sacrifices that cloud the face of heaven, anathema to the woman who strikes the cobblestones with her clogs!

"Lord, Lord, have the thunderbolts in your bronze palm vanished? You breathed the divine illness upon the holy body of our king and he falls to the ground, foaming like a snail and puffing like a turtle. Why? Why? What did he do to you? I ask you. Answer! Unleash a deadly affliction on all men, then, if you are just, and uproot the sperm from the loins of men and crush it on the stones!"

"Samuel!" thundered the Lord for the third time; "Samuel, be still and hear my voice!"

123

The prophet's body began to tremble; and as he leaned on the blood-soaked rock where God's sacrificial victims had been slaughtered, he heard all three of God's cries together, and raising his arms high he cried:

"Lord, here I am!"

"Samuel, fill your horn with prophetic oil and go to Bethlehem."

"It's far and my legs have rotted, beating the ground in your service for one hundred years now. Lord, mount another, I am no longer able."

"I am not speaking to the flesh, which I despise and never touch. I am speaking to Samuel!"

"Speak, Lord; here I am!"

"Samuel, fill your horn with prophetic oil and go to Bethlehem. Keep your mouth sealed, keep company with no one, and knock on the door of Jesse."

"I have never been to Bethlehem — and how will I know the door of Jesse?"

"I have marked it with a fingerprint of blood; knock on the door of Jesse and, of his seven sons, choose one."

"Which one, Lord? My eyes have grown dim and I cannot see well."

"As soon as you face him your heart will bellow like a calf; that is the one you shall choose. Part his hair, find the top of his head and anoint him king of the Jews; I have spoken!"

"But Saul will find out and ambush me on the way back and will kill me."

"And what do I care? I never valued the lives of my servants. Go!"

"I won't go!"

"Wipe the sweat from your face, straighten your jaws

so they don't quiver and speak to the Lord. You're stammering, Samuel; speak clearly!"

"I'm not stammering; I said I won't go!"

"Speak more softly; you're shouting as though you're
afraid. Why won't you go? Let Samuel condescend to
answer; are you afraid?"

"I'm not afraid; my love won't let me go. I anointed
Saul King of the Jews. I loved him more than my own
sons. I breathed my soul between his pale lips, the spirit of
prophecy, my spirit, and it glorified him. He is my flesh
and spirit; I will not betray him!"

"Why have you fallen silent? Has the heart of Samuel
emptied already?"

"You are omnipotent, Lord; don't play with me. Kill me!
You can do nothing more. Kill me!"

Samuel's eyes filled with blood. He hung onto the cliff
and waited.

"Kill me," his heart kept roaring inside him. "Kill me!"

"Samuel," the Lord's voice was gentler now, as though
entreating him.

But the old prophet kept growing fiercer.

"Kill me, there's nothing more you can do. Kill me!"

No one answered. The afternoon passed and the sun set.
A swarthy barefoot boy appeared. He climbed the footpath and approached the prophet with dread, as though
he were nearing the edge of the precipice. Placing the
prophetic meal at the foot of the cliff — dates, honey,
bread and a small pitcher of water — he hurried away
holding his breath and made his way down the slope to
the city and hid away in his father's cellar. His mother
bent down and embraced him.

"Still?" she asked, and her voice trembled. "Still?"

"Still," answered the boy. "He's still battling with the Lord."

The sun fell behind the mountain and the Evening Star appeared and hovered like a seed of fire over the sinful city. A pale woman saw it from behind her lattice and gave out a cry:

"Now it will fall and burn up the world!"

The stars spilled over the prophet's long hair; they played and sparkled, revolving obediently around an invisible wheel. And the prophet stood in their midst and trembled while they passed through his hair, beating at his temples like giant hailstones.

"Lord . . . Lord" . . . he whispered toward daybreak, and he could utter nothing more.

He took down the horn, filled it with prophetic oil, clasped his gnarled staff and descended the slope. His feet had sprouted wings and the dewdrops glistened like stars on his white beard. Two children were playing on the threshold of the first house and when they saw the prophet's mottled rags and green turban they took flight and began to scream.

"He's coming! He's coming!"

The dogs crouched in corners with their tails between their legs and a cow bellowed as she dragged her head on the ground. A strong wind swept through the city from one end to the other; doors slammed and mothers screamed and gathered their children in from the streets. Samuel beat his staff against the stones and passed with huge strides. "I feel like war over these people," he muttered, "like the plague; like the Lord!"

Two shepherds with long crooks appeared on the narrow path and as soon as they saw the prophet they fell to the ground. "Lord, command me to crush their skulls. Lord, speak to my heart; I am ready."

But no voice stirred in his mind and he passed, violently cursing the seed of man.

The sun scorched him, the dust swirled around his feet and enveloped him like a cloud. He thirsted.

"Lord," he cried, "give me water!"

"Drink!" answered a murmuring voice like a ripple of water beside him.

He turned and saw water trickling down the crevice of a rock and emptying in a ditch. He bent down, parted his beard and placed his mouth on the water. The refreshing coolness penetrated to the soles of his feet and his old bones creaked.

He returned to the road again; the sun set; he lay down at the foot of a palm tree, placed his right hand under his cheek and fell asleep. The jackals gathered round him, picked up his scent and fled in terror. The stars strung themselves over him like swords. He wakened at dawn and resumed the march. On the third day the mountain opened, the plain became visible and the Jordan glistened in its midst like a sluggish satiated serpent with green scales. Three more days passed and, suddenly, the stark white houses of Bethlehem glimmered behind the date trees.

A flock of doves passed over the prophet's head, hovering for a moment, and abruptly swooped toward Bethlehem in terror.

At the great northern entrance that reeked with the stench of the herd and teemed with blind and leprous beggars, the elders stood waiting for the prophet, trembling and mumbling among themselves: "Leprosy will fall upon the village! The Lord only descends upon the land to crush his creatures."

127

The eldest in the group braced himself and took a step forward.

"I will speak to him," he said.

The prophet arrived in a cloud of dust, his rags waving like a tattered flag of war.

"Peace or slaughter? What do you bring us?"

"Peace!" replied the prophet, extending his arms. "Go to your homes, empty the streets; I want to pass alone!"

The streets emptied, the doors were bolted. Samuel swept through the village, peering closely at the doors, passing his fingers over them. At the last house on the edge of town he discerned the fingerprint of blood on the door. He knocked. The whole house shook and old Jesse rose to his feet, terrified, and opened.

"Yero-Jesse,[23] peace to your house, health to your seven sons and may your daughters-in-law be blessed with male children; the Lord be with you!"

"May his will be done!" answered Jesse, and his lower jaw trembled.

A man appeared and filled the doorway. Samuel turned and saw him and his eyes rejoiced. The man was a giant, with curly black hair, a broad hairy chest and sturdy legs like bronze columns.

"This is Eliab, my first son," Jesse said proudly.

Samuel was silent, waiting for his heart to bellow.

"He must be the one," he said to himself, "surely he must be the one! Lord, why don't you speak?"

He waited a long time. Suddenly, the frightful voice burst out in him:

"Why are you muttering? Did your soul take a liking to him? I don't want him! I search out the heart, I probe the loins, I weigh the marrow in the bones; I don't want him!"

"Bring your second son," commanded Samuel, his lips turning pale.

The second son came, but the prophet's heart remained mute, his entrails unmoved.

"He's not the one! He's not the one! He's not the one!" he kept groaning, sweeping aside each of the six sons, one by one, piercing their foreheads, eyebrows and lips with his eyes, probing their shoulders, knees, waist and teeth as though they were rams.

Exhausted, he fell in a heap on the threshold.

"Lord," he shouted with anger, "you deceived me! You are always malicious and merciless and have no compassion for man. Come. I, Samuel, call you. Why don't you speak?"

Jesse approached, deeply shaken.

"There remains yet my youngest," he said. "David. He is keeping the sheep."

"Send for him!"

"Eliab," said the father, "go and call your brother."

Eliab knit his brows and the old man was frightened and said to his second son:

"Abinadab, go and call your brother."

But he, too, refused. They all refused.

Samuel rose from the threshold:

"Open the door. I will go myself!"

"Shall I describe the birthmarks on his body so you will recognize him?" asked the old man.

"No. I knew him before his father and before his mother."

Cursing, stumbling over the stones, he stormed up the mountain, shouting, "I don't want to! I don't want to!" as he proceeded.

And when he came upon a youth standing among his

sheep with a bright russet head glowing like the rising sun, Samuel stood still. His heart bellowed like a calf.

"David!" he called commandingly. "Come here!"

"You come here," answered David. "I will not leave my sheep."

"He's the one! He's the one!" roared Samuel, pressing forward with exasperation.

Coming close he grasped him by the shoulders, kneaded his back, examined his shanks, returned to the head.

"Who are you? Why are you searching me?" the youth demanded, wresting his head away.

"I am Samuel, the servant of God. He tells me to go and I go; he tells me to shout and I shout. I am his foot, his mouth, his hand, his shadow upon the earth. Bend down!"

He found the top of the youth's head and poured the holy oil on it.

"I despise you. I don't want you. I love another, but the wind of the Lord passes over me and, look, against my will I lift my hand and pour the prophetic oil upon the top of your head.

"David is anointed King of the Jews! David is anointed King of the Jews! David is anointed King of the Jews!"

He dashed the holy horn against the stones, where it shattered.

"This is how you've shattered my heart, Lord! I no longer want to live!"

Seven crows rushed from the depths of the heavens, they circled about him, and waited. The prophet unwound the green turban from his head and spread it on the ground as a shroud: the crows came closer, emboldened. He covered his face with the mottled rags and stirred no more.

"Uncle" Andreas is a unique man in a Cretan village. One day this "Uncle" Andreas gave me the definition of a lord: "A lord is a man who travels all over the world and then grabs a pistol and kills himself."

I've experienced most bitterly in my lifetime the horror of being obsessed by the longing to know other lands and people, and at the same time to be compelled to rush away and leave them behind. Great strength and inhuman discipline are required to endure this. The heart does not want to leave, it is enslaved in the warm personal details, it is caught up in people and things and cries out.

My heart was crying out this morning as I was saying farewell to the monastery: "Nevermore!" The raven of Edgar Poe was perched on my left shoulder like a clamp, shrieking. I said farewell to the splendid icons, to the cypress tree that rose solitary on the faraway cliffs, to the flowering orchard, the courtyard, the well . . . I said farewell to the people . . .

"Hold fast, old heart!" I kept muttering in Homeric verse. "You've known harsher pain!"

I descended the stairs and crossed the courtyard, accompanied by the archbishop, the prior and the sacristan. Pahomios appeared, wrapped in his blanket.

"Are you cold, Pahomios?" asked the bishop.

"I'm cold, Your Reverence!"

As he came forward to bid me farewell, he opened his blanket and gave me two small hot loaves of bread, branded with the seal of Saint Catherine.

"Aaron sends these to you for the road."

Taema was waiting for me with the camel outside the monastery. I said good-bye to the wonderful fathers. I shall never forget their heartfelt, noble hospitality. I squeezed Kalmouhos' hand. He was going to remain in

Sinai to work for a while longer; all this lofty landscape of the Old Testament has captured his heart. We parted: "God be with you!"

The return trip began. The divine colors of the desert gleamed, the mountains opened and we entered. Taema was singing softly in lullaby fashion, keeping beat with the slow rhythm of the camel, and I savored in silence, without haste, the wealth of the desert.

Night overtook us as we neared a date palm. We gathered wood, built a fire, brewed tea, boiled rice and ate. We lit our pipes and Taema's face glowed with every inhalation of the pipe — thin, swarthy — the Bedouin eyes flashed, small, bewitching like a serpent's.

For a moment we glanced at one another and smiled, but we were very tired and we lay down, one beside the other, and fell asleep.

We set out at dawn. The days and nights passed with the same divine rhythm. The mountains grew more fierce, wide green streaks were wedged in the red granite, the canyons grew narrower. At a ravine we caught a glimpse of a little water that shimmered for a second through the cane, palm trees and musk trees that were gathered around it. A herd of goats had aligned themselves on the stones and as we passed, the shepherdess, a young Bedouin girl, covered her face with her slender hands; but between her fingers two enormous eyes, like an animal's, flashed and played.

At noon of the last day we came out of the mountains. A rosy-hued unruffled expanse that looked like the sea stretched out before us for a considerable distance. We proceeded. This vast rosy expanse before us was not the sea, it was the desert, that a violent wind was whipping up into heated clouds of crimson.

We caught our breath as we entered the sandstorm. Taema's song ceased. Wrapping his white burnoose tightly around him he pushed forward.

The sand swept up and lashed at our faces and hands with stinging force. The camel kept spinning around, unable to keep its balance. The torturous journey continued for six hours; but I was secretly glad to be experiencing this abominable phenomenon of the desert.

Abruptly, the sea appeared just a step ahead of us. The houses of Raitho, children on the doorsteps, smoke rising from the rooftops. . . . Then, at the great gate of the monastery's dependency, the Archimandrite Theodosios — again that all-powerful alchemist of the human heart who, with love, transforms the desert.

I lived five of the most splendid days of my life in the small port of Raitho, awaiting the ship. I dipped into the sea, stretched out on the sand and roamed under the palm trees. On late afternoons, at the old biblical date palm, I watched the sparkling colors of the desert mountains being transformed faster than the eye could perceive — crimson, purple, azure.

A profound mystical agitation overtakes me as I walk along these Arabian shores in the desert. Old memories, from before my birth, stir silently on the threshold of my mind, like a shadow in Hades.

At times, forcing the ancestral memory within me to remember and shed light on my own particular existence, I think that I can divine the past. All my ancestors were born in a village of Crete to barbarians. When Nicephoros Phocas[24] took the island from the Arabs he crammed the infidel Saracens in some of the villages and these villages came to be named "Barbaroi."

And I like to imagine that my blood is not pure Greek

133

but that I am descended from the Bedouins. Some old ancestor once, following the half-moon and the green flag of the Prophet, jumped in the Arabian galleys that set out from Spain to conquer Crete — the island that flowed with milk and honey. And when he stepped ashore he dragged his ship with him on the sand and burned it so that there would be no hope of retreat and, thus, fighting under the shield of desperation, he forced the hopeless powers within him to win!

Walking along this Arabian seashore, I try to disentangle the inarticulate cries within me and distinguish the face of my ancestor.

Time passes and the heavens begin to hang out their enormous stars. By now Archimandrite Theodosios is uneasy and sends out some Bedouins to find me, tracing my steps in the sand.

We dine together at the small bountiful table, with Archimandrite Theodosios, and we talk. Infinite questions have been born to him here in the desert and he formulates them with great clarity and judgment. I speak to him about the great cities, about the contemporary agonies of man, about laborers, citizens, and about Russia.

Something Satanic breaks out in me; the serpent slithers up the tree of knowledge and hisses. Theodosios listens avidly.

"If you come out of your quiet cell, Father Theodosios," I say to him, "and pay heed to the world, your heart that is warm and loves mankind will shudder with anguish. A new excitement that did not exist before the war will seize you. A new, dark, religious terror.

"All peoples, after the war, are in ferment. A wind of devastation blows over the earth.

"The squall has broken through. It is coming. It will

sweep away many beloved countenances, many old ideas. There's no salvation."

"There's no salvation?" softly repeated the monk, looking at me with anguish.

"Only one: that we know it and be prepared."

Thus, disturbing the heart of the admirable hermit, transforming his serenity into gnawing unrest, I repaid his hospitality in the ultimate manner.

A LETTER

Dear Montita!

The dream is over — the date palms, the monasteries, the Bedouins, the desert are all behind me!

My arrival to this dark continent was like coming home. A mysterious agitation and murky recollection overcame me as I was breathing the blistering air and trodding the gray, insatiable sand.

Now, in reviewing this journey, I find three impressions affected me most profoundly:

(a). The boundaries between the green earth of the Nile and the sand.

(b). The necropolis of the Valley of the Kings in Thebes.

(c). The Sinai desert.

The boundaries. The last green leaf stands erect, with the entire desert before it, yet it resists and does not surrender. It gathers the last drop of moisture, crumbles the last bit of earth and rises, tiny, desperate and unyielding — this green leaf gave my heart the model of what is best in man.

I recalled the Roman fortress of Pompeii. All Pompeii was burning, the lava streaming down and covering it, and men and women were running about in a frenzy, clutching

136

their jewels and their children, rushing headlong to flee the city.

Only the sentry, standing erect at the post they had assigned him, at the outermost gates of the city, did not move, but calmly lifted his cape to shield himself from the suffocating smoke. And this is how he was found after eighteen centuries; erect, with his helmet and spear, and his mouth sealed.

The green leaf on the desert frontier rose before me exactly like this sentry and I thought with a shudder that this is our Obligation and this is the place of contemporary man.

At the Valley of the Kings I was horrified at the sight of man's vain effort to defeat death. The green leaf does not want to die.

In the dark, subterranean chambers of the yellow mountain, the mummy of the deceased lies like the cocoon of the caterpillar and waits for Spring to arrive so it can sprout its wings. All the clamoring procession of life bursts forth in green, red and yellow paint on the dimly lit walls surrounding the corpse. And the corpse — be he king or laborer — in the midst of the multicolored beloved shadows, himself a shadow, eats the shade, drinks the shade, cultivates the shadowy fields, crosses the shadowy river, sleeps with his shadowy wife and plays . . .

As I was wandering through the valley, Montita, this is how I saw the Earth, too, exactly like this valley. We are a shadow, we beget shadows, we huddle together for a brief span on the soil, then decompose and disappear. For whose sake have we performed the acts of war and love on this earth, and gone through the motions of men who eat, work, love an idea, cry and embrace one another?

Instead of an answer, our mouths are filled with a handful of dirt. What is our obligation? The quixotic, despairing campaign of the green leaf!

Trudging through the desert at the end of Sinai I felt my heart pounding rhythmically, obstinately like the pounding of the stonecutter on the stone. This is how those hearts that passed through the wilderness thirty centuries ago pounded and carved God on the granite. A people in the grip of hunger, fear and revolt, a people with voracious guts, a skin that trembled and a heart that resisted, created Jehovah, the God that matched them.

We find ourselves on an island. All this that we create with our senses and reflect upon with our mind is a small island made with a human brain and body, inside an infinite, barren, dark ocean. No matter where we begin, we always find the abyss at the end. We cry, shout, curse, turn back and start again on a new road, telling ourselves, at last this road has no end. But we always find the abyss at the end.

What is our obligation? To stand before the abyss with dignity. We must not cry out, nor laugh to hide our fear. Nor shade our eyes. Calmly, quietly, we must learn to look at the chasm without hope and fear.

This is the supreme cry of the desert. The contemporary face of the unfathomable is neither the tenderly sweet face of Jesus that blossomed in idyllic Galilee, nor the face of the tribal, merciless Jehovah that was forged in the Sinaitic wilderness.

New agonies have been born and man's soul has broadened with enlightenment and pain. Millions of human beings hunger and are wronged, and from their tormented bowels a new direction of life takes shape as always, a new

Response — a new face of the unfathomable. This face, if it is to succeed in comforting and captivating men, must resemble their face. It must be like the Laborer who is hungry, who works and rises up in revolt. This face must no longer be the leader of one tribe, but of the entire human race.

The "Exodus" *from the land of bondage* has begun. We cross the desert — we suffer, we grumble, we kill each other and create the new face of the Unfathomable, outside of every deity. But today's desert does not resemble this desert of Sinai. It is much harsher — filled with machines, cities and people.

Here in Egypt I shudder as I follow the "Exodus," the awakening, as the modern phrase goes, of a segment of the monstrous march. The Eastern peoples awaken, they organize, they exchange signals and set out.

Until now, the people in Egypt were submerged in the low, sunless strata of the animals: they labored, they hungered, they kept silent. Now the Exodus from the animal has begun: they have acquired a voice, are becoming enlightened and organizing. They have climbed to the next level — they have become property owners, merchants, small businessmen, and they have learned to read. They've expelled the foreigners who had been exploiting them. Some have risen even higher, uprooting everything. All the Asiatic and African peoples understand their brotherhood — and this is the most important reality of our time. Marching in the lead with them are all the people of Europe and America who suffer and are being exploited. The five continents and all the races — white, yellow and black — are in foment and stirring. And as always, a new world theory, contrary of course, to that of the leaders, goes be-

139

fore them like a cloud of smoke in the daytime and like a *pillar of fire* at night.

Crossing through the desert in Sinai, I saw the new "Exodus" of man. This vision, this mirroring of the desert, stands out as the most moving experience of my entire journey through the East.

That prolific grandfather the Nile, the fellaheen, the date palms, the tombs of the kings, the desert, the almond trees in bloom, the holy fortress of Saint Catherine, the reverent monastic rhythm, the cordial hospitality and kindness of the monks, the tolling of the bells at daybreak — I savored all these things and am still unsated.

The soul of man is the *burning but not consumed bush*. Nothing can extinguish it. And the mind of man is like the "small Scorpion" of an African legend. You'll like this Scorpion, Montita. It leaped within me throughout the journey!

The small Scorpion said: "I, the small Scorpion, will never invoke the name of God. Whenever I want to do anything I will do it with my tail!"

JERUSALEM

TOWARD THE
PROMISED LAND

The sea that was taking the worshipers to Jerusalem was calm; the sky with its flimsy clouds had a curious mysterious softness. The seacoasts of Greece, the islands, the sea gulls, the playful dolphins, the small birds that fluttered and chirped amid the ship's riggings — all had an exceptional warmth and charm for us today.

I look at my fellow-traveling pilgrims with curiosity. What kind of person is contemporary man who, after nineteen centuries, pursues and fulfills his deep longing to leave his home and begin the arduous and expensive journey to the East, in the midst of the Arabs, to worship at the unfathomable tomb of Christ?

They had come from all over Greece, in this sacred caravan; some with their luggage and hatboxes, others with simple bundles and baskets; and immediately upon boarding the ship they separated into two worlds, the one half on the deck and the other half in comfortable cabins and salons with untuned pianos.

I walked back and forth among these two worlds. Colorful blankets and greasy coverlets were spread out on ropes next to the ship's machinery; a cluster of old women had opened their baskets and were chewing away — the whole world smelled of red caviar and onions. A ruddy-cheeked old man with long flowing hair was sitting in the middle of all this, reading aloud the chronicle of Christ: his life, his Passion, how the Bridegroom went up to Jerusalem, afterward how they ate the bitter Last Supper, how the traitor disciple left in haste and how Jesus went up to the Mount of Olives and the sweat poured from his forehead *in drops of blood* . . .

The little old women in their black shawls were listening contritely, shaking their heads, sighing, and all the while, chewing away quietly, passively, like sheep. God was again becoming man in their simple hearts, was again being crucified on the terrifying cross and again saving mankind. An old man with his back toward the women was listening, stooped over his shepherd's crook, upon which he was carving a bird's head.

Suddenly, at the part where Christ, parched from thirst, cries out, "I thirst!" a plump, youngish woman sprang to her feet excitedly and with unendurable tenderness let out a cry, "My son!" — and my heart wrenched violently at the profound maternal cry of this woman who called even God her son.

Dusk of Holy Monday arrived. A tall, lean village priest rose, removed his priestly head covering, let his gray hair fall to his shoulders and began to chant the evening vesper service over the sea.

By the next day, Holy Tuesday, we had left the Aegean behind us and were entering Anatolia. To our right was the still indiscernible Africa, and to our left, beyond the horizon, Cyprus. The sea sparkled, serene and warm. Two black butterflies with red spots were flitting above the ship's ropes; a tiny famished sparrow that was following us swooped down and ate one of the butterflies; two squeamish young girls screamed and a man yelled: "Stop it — that's the way it's meant to be. What do you think God is, some delicate lady?"

I was approaching with deep emotion this sun-scorched land where once upon a time the flame leaped out of a tiny humble house in Nazareth and seared and rejuvenated the heart of man. I remember that other pilgrimage I had made to Moscow a few months ago, to the new Jerusalem of the modern, turmoil-ridden heart. Snow, endless silent steppes, crows and gray airplanes in the skies, and on the earth below antlike swarms of people, laborers and peasants hunched from work and anguish, all races, white, yellow, black, had come to worship at another Holy Sepulcher.

Today life finds itself in the same state of decay it was in two thousand years ago. But the problems that crush the equilibrium of the mind and heart today are harsher and more complicated and the solution more difficult and bloody. Then, a simple, unfathomably gentle voice emerged, and salvation shone on earth like spring. But today the word of Christ can no longer terrorize and put a rein on our soul and direct our actions. It has ceased to be effective. What does this mean? It has ceased to be true. When they say to the laboring masses (and today these masses are by necessity destined to find the new answer) that this earthly life has no value whatsoever and is only preparation for the future life after death, this sermon goes completely against our modern spiritual experience and our deepest contemporary needs. No one who is alive can believe this; therefore, this sermon has ceased to be true.

We are not concerned with what man's obligation was in past eras ("Obligation" meaning the form that man's encounter with God took) or what his obligation will be in the distant future. What is his obligation today? This is

145

the great agony. If God at one time took on the form of Dionysos, Jehovah, Christ, Ariman, and Brahmin, it is only of historical value today. His contemporary form is whatever wrenches our heart with blood and tears.

If the modern form of God that today's masses mold inside their factories and in their hovels and in their wronged hearts is to grab hold of them, he must resemble their own form. He must be like a Laborer who is hungry and works and no longer tolerates injustice but fights back. He must be a leader like the old Anatolians, with sheepskin on his feet and a double ax in his leather belt, a Ghenghis Khan who leads his hungry tribe and wants to plunder the cellars of the satiated and seize the harems from the impotent.

And now, what are we setting out to do in Jerusalem and what more do we have to talk about with the son of Mary?

At dusk, while the sun was sinking into the quiet waters behind us and the full moon was rising from the east, serene and melancholy like a golden death mask, the bishop solemnized on deck the divine service of Holy Tuesday. I had heard the passionate, erotic cry of Kassiani[25] to the Lord when I had chanced upon little mountain village churches in the springtime. The anguished womanly lament was sweetly enchanting as I listened, gazing through the small crossed window into the open country beyond. But tonight this female lament that so passionately cries out to God to save her from the male spilled onto the sea with unleashed grief. The sea incites the heart, it raises disturbances and questions that fresh green grass appeases. I was looking at the people around me. The well-dressed were unmoved, showing neither joy nor sorrow; they'd stand up, then sit down again, look at their watches. The poor in third class listened apart, and their faces shone. Their hearts were skipping, and for a moment their faces, hands and shabby clothing glowed. When this Holy Week, in which the Lord suffered like them passes, they will again fall back into the deadly daily darkness.

The moon had by now taken over the sky. Conversations were resumed; an old woman was telling her small granddaughter of the life and Passion of Christ. And the granddaughter was listening to the awesome story as though it were a fairy tale, tremblingly following the prince who was going to be killed. I, too, hiding in the dark, was listening, and it was the first time I understood the death march with such simplicity and such power. Rabbi Nachman,[26] the great unsophisticated founder of Hasidism, once said: "When I get an idea, so greatly do I work on it within me that, involuntarily, when I begin to tell it to others I see that it has ceased to be an idea and comes out like a myth. . . ." The same had happened now. Only the grandmother, that great simple heart, could so profoundly work all these futile theological sophistries within her and elevate them to a myth.

When I retired to my cabin and finally stretched out on my bed to sleep, I heard an unexpected conversation. Some fellow travelers were carrying on a heated discussion down in the ship's hold. One who, by the tone of his voice sounded very young, was vehemently enumerating with narrow-minded fanaticism the ignominy of our modern economic and social life — lies, thefts, injustices; the populace suffers, the great grow wealthier, women sell themselves, the priests have no faith; here, on this earth is where hell and paradise are; here is where we must demand justice and happiness, there is no other life. . . . Another was talking about Russia; in his excited imagination everything out there seemed right and holy. The fetishistic words "proletariat," "class struggle," "Lenin," rose from his entrails with apostolic fire, scorching his lips.

Cries could be heard, "Yes, yes, you're right! Fire and the ax!" Only one — I recognized the piercing voice of the deacon who was traveling with us — wanted to disagree; but his voice was drowned amid the shouts and laughter. The silent dance started suddenly to stir . . .

I leaped from my pillow and listened eagerly. In my imagination the hold of the ship was like a new catacomb where the modern-day slaves had gathered and were conspiring again to blow up the Earth. With difficulty I choked back the cry of joy. We were on our way to worship the familiar face of God, the gentle, martyred face full of promises, of future rewards after death. The little old women were carrying gifts to him: candles, silver offerings, fervent prayers; the unbelievers in first class above were quiet, free of care, and spoke of money and politics. . . . And down below, in the hold of the ship, we were hauling a formidable gift, the sperm of a new, unformed as yet, infant theogony.

I sensed again, deep within me, the transitory period we are living through. A sacred, cherished world is disappearing; another world, hard, brimming with blood, mud and fire, full of life, rises from the earth and the heart of man. It straddles all the ships and journeys on.

In the morning, through the milky mist, the Promised Land began to be discernible in the distance. At first just a line above the sea, then the low mountains of Judea appeared, gray at first, then soft azure and finally they drowned in the intense light of the day. Haifa seemed dark beside the blond spreading sand. To her left could be seen the new Jewish city Tel-Aviv, "the Crest of Spring."

A few famished sea gulls from the mainland flew over us, the butterflies on the ropes grew denser, the old women rose to their feet, collected their bundles, tied their black kerchiefs around their heads, crossed themselves and began to weep.

Sand, gardens, unctuous Arab women, wild fig trees, date palms. Automobiles sputtering as they climb to the Holy City. Hearts pounding loudly. And suddenly, sun-drenched and steaming, the stony, unsmiling vision is before us. Wharfs, battlements, fortress doors. White djellabas, green and red shawls, the scent of Eastern spices, rotted fruit and human sweat, fierce thousand-year-old cries, ghosts rising from the tombs, blood-soaked stones all crying out as they come to life.

JERUSALEM

I stand at the entrance of the Holy Tomb with bulging, insatiable eyes. It is Holy Saturday. The Church of the Resurrection is buzzing like an enormous beehive. Feverish,
bleary-eyed, Arab-shouting Christians, in fezzes and dirty
multicolored djellabas, are swarming over the tiles. Men
and women who have slept the night here are stretched
out on straw mats, rags or rugs, beneath the arches of the
church, waiting for the awesome moment now at hand,
when the divine light is going to leap out of the baldachin
of the Holy Tomb.

Gray water jugs with orange arabic motifs, soft drinks,
sherbets and lemons pass from hand to hand through this
human maze in the church encampment.

Coffeepots boil on portable burners under the great
icons; mothers bare their breasts in front of the crowds
and suckle their infants. A heavy, sour, human stench fills
the air; hot wax, oil and women's hair emit a nauseating
sheeplike smell. The rank odor of goats drifting up from
the Arab men is unbearable. Laughter, tears, shrieks. Some
are chanting, others are idling away the time with their
wives under the motley blankets in the dark corners of the
church; and as you pass through the heavy-scented darkness you catch sudden ripples of laughter coming from the
young girls who are being titillated.

An Abyssinian lord, lean and slender as a palm tree, strides through the crowds, wrapped in a green silk mantle; an Arab woman comes and kneels opposite me, fat, unctuous, with the dark eyes of a river animal. Her breasts hang flabbily and touch her stomach. Breath after breath comes wafting over me in a jumble of odors — some from wine and garlic, others from burning candles and frankincense. Now and then there is the unexpected fragrance of the divine April roses; you turn — a fellaha has just gone by carrying a rose to the Tomb.

Suddenly the sweating, black-haired throng swells into a stormy sea of worshipers. New Arabians are pouring into the courtyard with their six-winged cherubs and their lanterns and enormous candles, the size of their bodies. The rigid, indifferent English raise their canes to shield their heads. But the Arabians continue their frenzied shrieking. An old man, foaming at the mouth, climbs on the shoulders of the human maze and jumps from shoulder to shoulder waving two unsheathed swords in the air. He dances atop the shoulders, shrieking; only the whites of his eyes show, and the candles which coil around his waist are melting and dripping in the intense heat.

In a little while the Armenians descend upon the scene, their banners waving in the air; the young choir boys dressed in yellow shirts raise their fresh voices in the dense atmosphere. Next come the Copts, the Syrians, the Abyssinians, the Bedouin shepherds, the Maronites, five or six flaxen-haired Russians from the vast regions of Russia, and a few cold Americans, looking comical in this flaming Asiatic furnace. The women of Bethlehem come with their high cone-shaped headbands and their stark white shawls. An onslaught of multicolored waves, a brisk polemic rhythm, like the arrival of troops.

The church has overflowed with worshipers who have climbed up the columns and straddled the pews and are hanging over the women's section. All eyes, excited, ecstatic, are riveted on the center of the church, on the small baldachin which the Patriarch has already entered, and out of which, any second now, the divine light will leap forth.

A fellah, whose head is tightly bound with strips of camel hair, jumps upon the shoulders of an Arab, waving a huge white taper with red ribbons in the air and frenetically starts calling out to Christ to emerge. The masses, all in a body, go wild. Swarthy arms thrash about, the silver bracelets on the arms of the women jangle, their henna-painted nails glisten like droplets of blood. All the Anatolians — Arabs, Bedouins, Abyssinians — heads craning upward, are shouting, laughing, sighing. A young man faints and soldiers lift his wooden body and lay it in the courtyard. A lean old Maronite priest, dressed in a stark white robe and red sash, falls on the tile floor, foaming at the mouth; and in a sudden surge a mob of old women, their arms and chins tatooed with crosses, mermaids, and quotations from the Bible, fling themselves upon him . . . they press forward, shrieking, and touch the epileptic. In their primitive souls they think that an awesome invisible power has suddenly descended upon this convulsed body.

The huge marble slab that covers the ground where Christ was laid after his removal from the cross is licked and worn away from the kisses. For centuries, the human masses have been falling all over it, kissing and eroding it. They touch the marble lightly with their palms and then rub their face and neck three times. If every thousand centuries, says Buddha, a peacock feather is passed over a granite mountain, the day will come when the mountain will be eroded away and will disappear. Similarly, the in-

numerable feet of the faithful have worn away the tiles of
the church and the courtyard, the Tomb of Christ, the cliff
of Golgotha, the Stone the angel rolled away; all have
been eroded by the lips of the people.

An orthodox priest next to me looks with yellow hatred
at the Copts, the Latins and the Armenians. He bends over
and speaks to me with a choked voice:

"This entire church belongs to us, the Orthodox. All the
sacred shrines are ours. The heretics, whom God has
damned, want to take them from us; but we're fencing off
the disputed areas with iron bars and won't let anyone set
foot inside! Look at what we gave the Abyssinians, a rock.
Come what may, we're not giving them another inch. Now
we're going to throw the Armenians out; they've over-
stepped their boundaries and are standing on our ground.
Whatever the Latins tell you is a lie. All their shrines are
fakes. I hope to God the day comes when we can throw
them out!"

"I hope to God the day comes," I answered, "when your
hearts will fill with love. When the divine light no longer
comes down to your candles but into your dark, anti-Christ
mind!"

A wave of fellaheen passed between us and separated
us. They were sticking their tongues out, whistling, laughing; their eyes were corroded from trachoma, their teeth
were gleaming white. The men were tall, lean, nimble-
bodied; the women were fat, ugly, their foreheads tightly
wound with ropes of copper coins; their lips glistened ebul-
liently.

But now a sweet melody is heard from the altar. The
ushers are beating rhythmically on the tiles with their long
silver-handled canes; they slowly advance and open a path.
The children's choir moves forward, the metropolitans and

153

bishops follow in their gold vestments. The Patriarch, with his snow-white beard, enormous weary eyes and stark-white, long tapered fingers, appears on the threshold . . .

The litany begins, the bells toll, a violent wind of sanctity and frenzy blows over the multicolored heads. I feel once more the warmth of the almightiness of the heart of man. Hands reach upward, feet dance, the heart leaps and cries out to the Savior. The air fills with an invisible presence. Surely, if the priests and cultured people had not been present in the church the fellaheen would have resurrected Christ. They would have forced him to condense in the air and come down to earth, no longer as an idea or a phantom, but in the form of flesh and voice. They would give him fish and honey and he would eat. They would touch him and their hands would be filled. And when he'd walk, the tiles would echo. "God had no ear," says an Indian philosophy. "God could not hear; but man, who was in pain, cried out and God was compelled, by force, to create an ear to hear the woes of man."

Looking at the fellaheen today, I understood in what manner the heart of man created heaven and earth. It brought down the invisible powers and dressed them in flesh and gave voice to mute infinity.

The Patriarch bent down and entered the holy baldachin of the Sacred Tomb alone. A hush fell over the trembling, multitudinous throng. Mothers raised their infants to their shoulders so they could see, the fellaheen gaped with mouths drooping, the Europeans raised themselves on tiptoe and stared with curiosity. The seconds were falling thickly on our heads; the air strained and cracked like the skin of a drum. And all at once a brilliance leaped from the low door of the Sacred Tomb; the Patriarch emerged holding a big cluster of white lit candles. In a flash, from floor to ceiling, the church flooded with flaming candles. Everyone had surged toward the Patriarch to receive the light. Some were carrying thick white tapers and others held thirty-three white candles. They put their hands in the flame and quickly rubbed them over their faces and breasts. They poured out into the courtyard, their hands curled around the flame of their candles, and ran to their homes.

The church emptied. All this stupendous din, the frenzied throngs and the motley rags seemed like an outlandish, improbable dream. But as I bent down, in the course of my lonely wandering in the church, I knew that all this Anatolian vision was real; because there on the tiles I saw the remains of the awesome apparition: pumpkin seeds, orange peels, olive pits and broken pop bottles.

PASCHA

I stroll through the brightly lit Church of the Resurrection the afternoon of Easter and the scattered, trampled lemon flowers fill the air with the scent of citrus and decay. A little old woman is kneeling before the stone marking the Descent from the Cross, and her pale daughter, standing by, is handing items of her dowry to her, one by one. Pathetically, the aged mother passes them over the shiny stone, murmuring ancient secret exorcisms. The thick, tightly sewn nightshirt that will become the bridal gown, the Anatolian rose-colored stockings, the pillowcases, the sheets, the towels, the copper bracelets and silver dangling earrings. . . . The young woman, unmoved, indifferent, like an animal whose time has not yet come, takes the sanctified dowry items back from the aged hands and pats them flat in a yellow woven traveling bag.

Frankish priests pass by hurriedly; sweaty, unwashed Armenians with hawkish noses, and lean Abyssinians pause at the icons, their dried-out bodies smelling like roasted corn.

Standing under an arch between two columns is a youngish Arab priest, thin, small-boned, with a sparse dark beard. He is resting his chin on a long cane staff and staring down at the tiles with unmoving eyes. A young Arab woman, wrapped in a black robe and holding a white Easter candle, stands next to him, crying. She, too, is slender, with large eyes. She is speaking gently, amicably, to the young priest, without looking at him. I leaned against the column and listened for a long while to the mysterious lamentation of this woman, as though I were hearing a water vein flowing hopelessly over smooth pebbles toward the sea. I have never before felt a woman's heart melting with such pathos, flowing with such resignation toward the male.

This was my only deep Easter joy today. In vain I paced back and forth in the church, feeling absolutely no resurrection within me. I remembered Mount Athos; I remembered my intense commitment to believe.

I had gone to Mount Athos to quiet my heart, to see the desert in bloom, so that at night, at the hour when the sun sets, I, too, could welcome the Lord at my doorstep. Undisciplined fires burned in me, unspeakable eroticisms toward woman, God, ideas; I couldn't distinguish between them because none of my desires would take on a solid form. I wanted to torment and transform within me, as best I could, all the natural forces, the old legacies and the new passions. "Ah, Love and Silence will give me everything," I thought — "the two primeval forces that assisted God in the hour of creation."

"Ah! to remain alone, free, far from the treadmill of society, outside the sheepfold of the human herd! To walk, and walk, and see nothing but the sun, the sea and the rocks. To feel my guts stirring like two forked leaves on the great tree of God!"

The Byzantine monasteries appeared before me, high above the waves, dazzling and cool, like pebbles that have just emerged from the water, still dripping. At the seashore

157

nearby, monks were stooped over, tugging at a dragnet filled with fish; a little way off, a boat had been pulled into the shipyard and, with its oars resting across its bosom, was lying stretched out on its moorings, bathing in the sun.

What a miracle! what solitude! what blessedness! I thought, as I climbed. And when I entered the first monastery and stepped over the old, worn threshold and proceeded to the outer courtyard, a mysterious warmth overtook me:

"Lord," I cried silently, "whoever you are, help me to elevate my spirit above joy and happiness! To pursue the supreme hierarchy of pleasure, the path of self-denial and pain!"

The dusky, cool church was filled with saints and angels; stone doves on the tops of the columns, intertwining letters, rams' heads and vines with thick stone grapes. I felt surrounded by invisible presences, cherubim and seraphim were sliding down from the cupola and gropingly touching me.

The eyes of the Virgin Mary shone in the cool darkness, large, compassionate, grieving, and her strong chin glowed in the dim incense-laden air.

I stood before her and spoke:

"*Glykofilusa*,[27] Lady of the Sea. Oh, heart of mankind, who contained Him whom heaven and earth cannot contain. O deed, O Tenth Muse, O Virgin Mary the crier, you carried the cry of danger like the frontier sentry who perceived from afar the swarming Arabs trampling the divine light.

"And you arose as Commandress, lightly brandishing your *apelatiki*,[28] and the *yerakokoudouna*[29] and your silver *tsaprassia*[30] rang out, and your chaste breast gleamed like the Full Moon.

"And all the young men leaped up, ripe for the pleasure of God and Death and surged behind you, Amazon!

"Because you stir in my heart like a Christian Nike who doesn't fear blood and follows, with long clanging strides, the militant God on earth!"

Thus spoke my heart and it danced as I wandered from monastery to monastery. I wanted to choose the most austere of them all so that I, too, could perfect my asceticism. For a short time, a long time, forever, I didn't know. I only knew that I must remain completely alone, and silent for months.

They assigned me to the monastery of Prodromos,[31] an isolated monastery above the sea, wedged against a precipice, desolate, without water and trees. A narrow footpath wound up the slope from the seashore and, after an hour's walk, reached my doorstep. I had two cells and an old ruin of a chapel covered with frescoes. Prodromos was standing next to Christ in the icon to the right of the iconostasis. He looked like a grasshopper, slender and green, with two enormous yellow eyes; one would think, by the way he was standing on the edges of his feet, that he wasn't walking, but jumping from tree to tree. Behind his shoulders, like two giant tongues of flame, two enormous wings sprouted; this lean, dried-out body looked like it had caught fire and was burning; had caught fire and was leaping up to burn the whole world.

I spent the first few days bent over my threshold planning my asceticism. With figures, with logical sequence, with geometrical madness.

I would divide myself into two camps: the upper and lower, the illumined and the dark, the soul and the body.

159

And I'd wage war between them. "I will subdue as best I can the desires of the flesh," I reasoned. "Does it want to sleep? I will stay awake. Does it want to eat? I will fast. Does it want to rest? I will get up and climb the mountain. Is it cold? I will bare my body and walk among the rocks."

And little by little I was aiming at higher prizes: "When I conquer the flesh I will turn to the soul and divide it, too, into two camps; lower and higher, human and divine. I will fight the small intellectual joys — books, art, logic and learning. I will fight the established, acknowledged virtues — justice and mercy, friendship, patience and reverence."

And again, if I won a second time, I aimed in my mind toward a new severance: "Down with Hope, the final enemy, and up, high, with the flame of God that will be consuming me, in profound darkness, without reward!"

I shall never be able to describe my torment and its inexpressible sweetness. After three months I could no longer stand up from the fasting and hardship. My eyes were sunken, my ears buzzed, my arms and legs had become like the grasshopper's.

Thus, in such agony, the days and nights passed. Suddenly one morning, without my having yet made any decision, a derisive voice welled up inside me:

"You're leaving!"

Spitefully, I answered back:

"I don't need your permission! Yes, I'm leaving."

"Playactor! You're so frightened and lazy, you refuse to face your soul without shouts and rhetoric. You're leaving! It's more comfortable down there; here you were cold and hungry; you saw no one and no one saw you — and what value does virtue have without an audience? And what kind of actors are we if we don't have admirers to applaud us? Ugh! I'm disgusted to be stuck with you!"

"Who are you?"

"I am the Eye that vigilantly culminates in your guts and watches. And like it or not, whether you're moving forward or going backward, in your ruin and in your salvation, I walk with you relentlessly!"

"I don't want you! I'm human, flesh and mud and spirit, all in one! And all of me, reaching to my heart, to my forehead and on, upward, is burning! Solitude doesn't calm my heart, Christ can no longer save my soul, a stern voice calls me and I follow it. I'm not playacting and I don't want an audience."

"I don't ask you! I'm inside you, I'm the horseman riding you. Only I don't pass away, and you will leave, ephemeral plaything of water, earth, fire and wind! I, only, exist!"

"Who are you?"

"I'm with you so many years, wretched man, and you don't know me?"

Thus, derisive and grieving, the voice faded away.

THE MOSQUE
OF OMAR

The two great Annunciations, the Christian and the Greek, sparkle in my mind and unite in a mystic synthesis:

In the one, the ethereal, vigorous Angel swoops down from heaven with a lily in its hand; and the Virgin, fascinated and trembling, turns with her whole body toward the door that has just opened. In the other Annunciation, the Swan, a dazzling creature, rises from the muddy waters and anchors itself intimately in the age-old custom on the female body. And the woman bends with abandon and horror over the long swaying neck, the palms of her hands raised beseechingly, like a creature in pain and ashamed, but unable and unwilling to resist the animal . . .

Today I saw a third Annunciation: the angel does not descend from heaven nor does the animal rise from the muddy waters; upon this earth, ardently and humanly, man brings the "good news" to woman.

I walk around the Mosque of Omar and my heart beats carefree, like a kid on the cliffs. I don't stretch my body toward heaven — this earth looks good to me. This country of mine is made especially for my soul and my body. I am reminded of another day when I was wandering, tired and restless, in Kurd-besieged Eriban, in the heart of Armenia. The doors were bolted, the streets deserted, the women and children wailing behind the heavy shutters. I wandered alone, full of agony and exasperation. And suddenly, in the midday heat of the burning sun, another sacred mosque unexpectedly rose before me, covered from the foundation to its cupolas with green and blue porcelain and coral flowers. My blood at once grew calm, my mind rejoiced, and as I sat beneath the pointed Arabic arch in the cool shade all seemed good and right to me and death but a cool shadow after a blistering march.

Similarly today, after upholding the Christian ideal to scorn the earth and leave it behind, this Mosque of Omar comforts and reconciles my heart with the soil. It gleams brilliantly in the sun, sparkling, joyful, multicolored, like a gigantic male peacock.

I stride hurriedly across the great square over the ancient quays of Jerusalem. I walk around the magnificent mosque for hours, delaying as long as possible entering the dark door and plunging into the refreshing cool marvel. I look through the embrasures at the surrounding vision of Jerusalem. Beyond, the Moab Mountains steam gently, they sway slightly and shimmeringly disappear in the sun. The Mount of Olives is before me, parched, thirsty, covered with dust; and below lies the city, eroded by the burning sun, its bald houses with their black window holes resembling skulls. Camels pass, one behind the other, swaying rhythmically, indestructible, as though they had set out thousands of years ago . . .

This is the peak, I reflected, upon which Jehovah stood with distended nostrils, accepting the sacrifices and smelling the blood. Here is where the great Temple of Solomon rose, impenetrable fortress of the stiff-necked God; and I relived all its bloody, hate-filled, polemic history. The hard, sunburned heads, the hawk nose, the narrow unrelenting forehead, the rigid neck, the burning rapacious eye of the Hebrew race.

But as I was wandering through this bloody cesspool of Israel, I turned. The Mosque of Omar was rising in the sun, like a fountain of sculpted precious stones, climbing, playing a little in the air, circling, giving way and coming back to earth. It did not want to leave.

I approached fascinated. The Arabic letters, plaited like flowers, were turning into maxims of the Koran, intertwining like creeping vines on the columns, blooming, grasping the dome. Thus they embraced and captivated God in the blooming, wild vineyard of earth.

My eyes were refreshed as I crossed the threshold and plunged into the multicolored, mysterious shade of the temple. At first, as I came in from the raw light, I could not distinguish anything. Only a sweetness spilled over me and relieved me, like a bath; first my body and, immediately after, my mind. I walked on, trembling with joy and anticipation. This is how the faithful Moslems must walk in the dark, after death, in the cool paradise of righteous recompense.

I moved ahead with arms outstretched and little by little my eyes became adjusted. The windows rose before me like constellations, the dome, all gold and emerald, softly filled with light; the details began to appear, dancing ahead in the azure shadow — the lines, the decorations, the quotations from the Koran that were lying in ambush like insatiable, amorous eyes, behind profusely flowering branches and ethereal animals.

A believer, kneeling on a straw mat with his face turned toward Mecca, was praying. He remained for a long while with his forehead touching the ground, trustingly, like an infant on its mother's bosom. Then slowly he lifted his head, sat up and gazed high into the golden green strip of the dome. His eyes ecstatically pursue the hidden, slippery quotation of Mohammed in the midst of the intricate lines and patterns. As though in a dream pursuing the mysterious doe. And what joy when he finally understands that all these narrow, intertwining lines are not an idle game of fantasy but a high, austere commandment of the Prophet!

Only the believer can distinguish and fit together the unmatched difficult outlines, integrating the great message into a mystical synthesis in his heart. He does not scorn the apparent, nor does he seek the essence beyond the apparent; nor does he restrict himself only to the visible palpable world, without yearning for anything more. The phenomena are what create the essence. All this life — water, bread, woman, mountains and animals — are γράμματα[32] (outlines and games); and joy to the heart that can fit them together and find the phrase to grasp the meaning.

Christ commands: "Scorn the earth and its riches. Beyond the phenomena is the essence, beyond this transient life shines immortality." Apollo stands firm on the marble and commands: "Harmonize your heart with the earth, calmly rejoice in the ephemeral, solid order of things; outside the harmony of your mind is chaos." And Buddha, with his deep, seductive, serpentine eye, looks at us smilingly, finger in mouth, and drags us into chaos.

Today, inside the Mosque of Omar, wanting to discipline the anxieties of my heart, I struggle to harmonize whatever I love deeply in this world: the sober mind and burning imagination, geometric solidity and precision, and at the same time, not beyond, but within, the mystical flame of anxious yearning. I gaze at the dome of the mosque for hours, like a believer: the Arabic capers transform the animals and plants into decorations, the decorations into letters, and they uncover God — and we see him as we see a lord through the thick foliage of his garden.

I sit in a corner of the mosque, on the straw mat, overcome by an indescribable sweetness. The rigid, austere outline of the Parthenon suddenly looms in my mind. Similarly, the pure divine countenance of Beatrice must have risen in the mind of Dante at the moment he was surrendering, exhausted, to the warm, earthly embrace.

I know you have always served as a lesson in balance, hardness and discipline in a rhythm superior to me. You set limits to my desires, you set a barrier around the disorderly energies of my youth. You found concise words without tenderness, commanding, like orders to an athlete in order to open a path for me. In the beginning you seemed to me the rigid achievement of abstract thought, and my heart did not want to follow you. But little by little, in time, with love, I understood. You revealed yourself to me like an airy ripple, subordinated to the straight line; a violent passion which from its abundant strength binds itself to a superior health, a geometry pulsating like music. And slowly I understood, sitting at your feet, O Parthenon, that serenity is the resultant of all storms. That the highest mission of man is in faithfully continuing the formless struggle of matter, to liberate it by subordinating it to solid human form.

For the first time on this earth, it seemed to me the chaos of the heart subordinated itself with such grace, and without renouncing its riches, to the austere outline of the mind. The victorious mind, assembling infinity on a dry, sunbaked skull-like cliff, gave it a broader kingdom to rule. Just as, when in the midst of chaos, man finds the law that governs a series of phenomena and strictly encloses it in the Word and the world becomes calm and the contradictory forces are regulated, similarly in the anarchy of natural forces, the Parthenon rises soberly and legislates the chaos.

But today, recalling this victory of logic, constriction and rage beleaguer my soul. My heart is not pure, my mind has shattered the old equilibrium. Today, whatever balance holds the rebellious forces in divine serenity seems foreign to me, narrow and false, and I do not understand it. Great concerns have been born, Lucifers have risen from the earth with arms full of dangerous gifts, with lips that twitch from smiles that are inscrutable, mocking, perplexing. The helmet of Athena has shattered and no longer can hold the head of the world.

An irresistible instinct urges me to dig under the foundations of the serene temple. I know this unsparing marble syllogism has its foundations in the passionate Caryatids, with the high, agitated breasts, the painted lips and dark, dangerous eyes.

With difficulty I struggle to make clear my emotions. The contemporary Caryatids who convulse our souls do not have the enchanting visage of this ancient harem. They look more like the Furies and the Fates. One is called Hunger and she walks ahead and countless men follow her. Aphrodite never had so many lovers as this sallow, flat-chested, unsmiling, unconquered Amazon. The others are called Revenge, Rage, Freedom.

What Parthenon, what mosque, will be built upon these Caryatids? I sit in this cool corner of the mosque and realize that all my joy has left me. Life has become oppressively heavy. Today, every moment that passes cannot satisfy us, either with its joy or with its sorrow. We push it aside roughly, in haste to see the next moment.

In another age, man would surely be happy to continue to remain in the austere certainty of the Parthenon; or to sit cross-legged and glorify God in the cheerful Mosque of Omar that exudes a faith of flesh and aroma. Today, the heart beats impatiently, it cannot be contained, it fights to make distinctions — and more important, to participate in building the future temple of its as yet faceless, fermenting God.

THE LAMENT
OF THE HEBREWS

I pass hurriedly through the dark covered streets of Jerusalem. The Hebrew eyes gleam sarcastically, restlessly, covetously; the Moslems are calm, deeply confident in Allah's care; they watch you with indifference and aloofness as you rush by.

I hurry through this dense, human maze, fascinated by the colors, scents and din of dirty, wonderful Anatolia. I am anxious to reach the ruins of the wall of the Temple of Solomon, where for over eighteen centuries now, the Jews lament their lost country and call on Jehovah to come down and again glorify his temple.

The sun is finally setting as I pass through filthy narrow streets; for an instant a crimson glow floods the archways under the vaults, like a stream of blood issuing from the setting sun. The dark, slight Arabic faces take on a metallic gleam and for a moment even the cheeks of the pale Jews acquire a ruddy flush.

As I turn the corner I notice two elderly rabbis walking hastily ahead of me. They are dressed in the most improbable, ostentatious coats; one is a canary yellow velvet and the other a lush green. These two old men shine like stars in the dimly lit dirty streets of the Hebrew quarter. I follow them, surmising they have dressed in their formal

169

vestments to appear before their God at the ancient ruins and begin their lament.

We walk down the slippery, cobbled streets and suddenly I hear a synchronized wailing chant of male voices. I stop, fascinated. The dirge sounds so sweet to me, soft, persistent, like spring rain, an intermingling of tears and laughter. I walk on a few paces and find myself before the renowned wall, the only remnant of the Temple of Solomon. A very commonplace wall, with heavy stones, set without asbestos cement. Up high the stones are covered with moss and down below, as high as people could reach, the stones have been worn away by the handling, the kisses and caresses of the Jews.

About fifty worshipers, Old Testament in hand, are leaning on the wall, wailing. A rabbi with coarse whiskers, wearing a black silk robe and heavy fur cap on his head, is swaying back and forth from the waist, chanting rhythmically, monotonously, through his nose. There's a young man next to him shouting. Another, with a greenish black redingote, a hard hat and yellowish goatee, has removed a rope of hair from his waist, belts it over his redingote and begins to rock back and forth. An old man is crying silently with his face pressed against a crack in the wall.

They keep coming, they kiss the walls, rub their faces on the stones, breathe deep sighs. A hunchback dwarf with a red fez, a black turban and a raven-black shiny beard paces back and forth despondently. There are rabbis in orange-colored mantles, others in blue, white, violet — like has-been old actors. The faithful cluster around them and begin their droning lamentation. Two children, about eight or ten years old, begin to cry as they kiss the lower part of the wall, and the dwarf approaches them and begins to cry, too.

The women stand in a corner at the left. A young girl with curly, jet-black hair, a yellow shawl, long dangling earrings and painted lips leans against the wall and looks sideways, smiling at the men. Her eyes are still red from crying but she is relieved now and the force of youth has overtaken her. She has forgotten the divine curse, the devastated temple, the Diaspora and the martyrdom of her race and looks at the men with erotic, covetous eyes. She well knows that only love can save her generation and multiply the Jews and rebuild the Temple of Solomon.

But the old men and women weep. I live through this strange moment with indescribable agitation. An old man is trying to tear himself away from the wall but cannot bear to leave, and falls upon it once more. The Jews have gathered here from the four corners of the Earth, to merge and weep together. They have come from Galicia with their long redingotes and curls that dangle at their temples; from Arabia in their white djellabas, from Poland, short and red-haired; from Babylonia, tall and majestic like biblical Patriarchs; from Russia, Spain, Greece and Algiers. A man who looks Chinese, with a sparse, turned-up mustache, sits cross-legged, moving his head and upper body rhythmically, slowly, mournfully reading without stopping, like a tired weeping child.

The curse of the terrifying God falls upon all these heads. *And I shall ravage them, and give them to eternal ruin and lamentation and mockery. And remove from them the voice of joy and the voice of gladness, the voice of the bridegroom and the voice of the bride, the scent of myrrh and the light of the lamp.* They were scattered over all the Earth in sunless Jewish ghettos. In the Middle Ages high walls separated them from the rest of the city. The doors opened in the morning and closed at night. They wore a

171

mark of disgrace, a strip of red or yellow cloth on their shoulder, breast or head. In northern medieval France they wore a yellow cap, in Germany a hood and cap of red or green. This was so that their tormentors could single them out and abuse them or beat them with impunity. And when they would take them up to the pyres they dressed them in a black robe, embroidered with crosses and flames of hell and demons, and this is how they walked through the chanting crowds who cursed them.

In the throes of their dishonored life and martyrdom of death, this simple wall, eaten away from all the kisses, gleamed before them like a high bronze shield. On the snow-covered steppes of Russia, or sunbaked Spanish plains, Zion, "the acme of virtues," rose up in their cries like a heavenly rainbow. For over eighteen centuries now they weep with their face turned toward this wall, and they call out: "Lord, Lord, behold our misfortune! Others have seized our inheritance, strangers have taken our homes. We must buy the water we drink and the wood for our fires. Joy has left our hearts, our dance has changed and become mourning, the crown has fallen from our heads!"

This is how the Hebrews lament these many centuries, searching out, caressing, kissing the ancestral stones. Uprooted, without land, they roam the earth. Their great leader is no longer Moses the lawgiver and general, but the ragged, homeless, inconsolable Wandering Jew.

For so many centuries now they have been sending representatives, the poor, the aged, the laughingstock of all nations, to this wall so that Jehovah could see to what depths his Chosen Race has fallen and that it is finally time for him to remember and to keep his word. Had he not promised them all the Earth? Had they not remained faithful for thousands of years? Had they not been dishonored, killed, martyred, for his sake? How long must they wait? So ask the envoys, and cry out for their rights. They are like lenders who have loaned out their tears and love at interest, and God is the debtor. The Hebrew usurers demand, unremittingly, with tears and exasperation, that they be paid.

The Jewish spirit wants to conquer the Earth, to subordinate all nations to its rhythm, to crush the present, because the Earth cannot contain it and smothers it. This is its profoundest characteristic. The Greeks love to harmonize opposite forces, they rejoice in and easily fit into every ephemeral moment. They brought balance to the world. The Jews battle ceaselessly to upset the balance and agitate the heart of man. Reality can never contain them; beyond each ephemeral moment they demand the absolute.

THE PROMISED LAND

The sun had finally set; the star of Aphrodite and Astarte glittered, suspended over the dark blue mountains of Judea. The rabbis closed their books, at peace with themselves, their aged hands slowly, falteringly caressing the wall as they filed out. In their imagination the temple had been rebuilt. Zion had risen again, completely new, and the Messiah entered once more through the fortress door of David, as tradition would have it, *on a white ass.*

A Hebrew friend was with me, a modern atheistic adventurer who was all efficaciousness and logic. He turned to me and, nodding ironically, said:

"They think that their shouts in the air are going to rebuild Jerusalem. Only mass production and the just distribution of wealth will create a perfect mankind — the new Jerusalem."

"Comrade," I answered, peevishly, "these voices that you ridicule are always the forerunners that sow seeds in the air. After a thousand or two thousand years you sociologists, you laborers of logic, come along and reap. The mystical preparation of reality has always been this way. The heart suffocates, cries out and wants to escape; it becomes a voice and storms the air; it finds other hearts; it sets the brains and hands into motion and mobilizes the visible and invisible powers. This is the only way the word can become flesh and walk the earth.

"What does it need to become flesh? Only this: to have its cry sustained in the air for many years . . ."

I heard this cry — the Source — throughout the many weeks that I wandered through Judea. My eyes burned from looking at the steaming desert. From Jerusalem to the Jordan and the Dead Sea, four hundred meters below the sea level of the Mediterranean, not a single flower grows, not a drop of water rises from the parched earth. The mountains are desolate, austere, inaccessible. Perfect for an artist who loves the abstemious tragic beauty of this world. Perfect for the prolific procreation of prophets inside their ascetic nakedness. But for simple, virtuous people who want to build houses, plant trees and have children, all this smoldering, silent wilderness is unbearable.

A light, azure flash of madness hotly licks your mind as you pass through these uninhabited gray mountains, without a bird or a single green leaf. Only the unexpected sound of a hungry crow fluttering overhead or the howl of the jackals close by at night as they dig in the sand.

Jericho smiles for a moment before you, like an oasis. Orchards of blooming pomegranates, banana trees, fig trees, mulberry trees, surrounded by tall, slender date-palm trees — charming as Ionic columns or gushing water spouts. Your eyes and body are rested and refreshed. But quickly the oasis disappears as though swallowed by the sand.

The same pleasantness surrounds Haifa, with her renowned orchards brimming with orange and lemon trees. And below, in Hebron, the ancient town of Abraham, the earth is tranquilly tamed by the plowshare of man.

In Samaria and Galilee the mountains take on a more

hospitable appearance. Birds, water and trees domesticate the landscape. But fevers from the mire kill the people. "Even a bird flying overhead will die," says an old Arabic parable.

In biblical times Palestine flowed with milk and honey and the grapes were so heavy that two men were required to lift them. Today, Palestine's appearance is unrecognizable. The Arabs have brought their ancestral desert with them.

Yet a new breath, the ancient Jewish spirit, blows in again over the devastated plains and valleys of Palestine. The Jews are back, plowing the land, channeling the waters, planting, building. They fight in the noblest manner, fructifying the earth in order to conquer her. They fight to bring a little light and sweetness and joy to their fallowed country.

A Jewish rabbi in one of the new agrarian communities was speaking to me:

"Each man has a certain set of things he must free: his animals, his land, the tools of his trade, his body and his brain. He has a duty to liberate all these. How? By using them and cultivating them. If he does not liberate them he cannot liberate himself. Likewise, every people has a certain periphery — lands, traditions, ideas — that it must set free, if it wants to be free. The Jewish people have Palestine."

We walked along the broad, dusty road bordering the Valley of Josephat at the foot of the Mount of Olives. The tombstones on the Jewish graves, deeply imbedded in the ground, were drowned in the glaring noonday light. The little village of Gethsemane, just two paces ahead, was blotted out in darkness, so blinding was the brilliance of the sun. Unexpectedly, there among the graves, two camels filed silently by, one behind the other, their necks swaying slowly. For a moment their patient black eyes, with the long lashes, gazed at us gently and my heart lightened as I felt the presence of a warm living thing moving through this inhuman wilderness.

Walking and breathing easily beside me in this furnace was a young Jewess, a teacher named Judith, who had come to show me a garden for Jewish children. She was about twenty years old, short, lissom, with hooked nose and restless jet-black eyes. Her hair was curly and coarse, her chin broad, firm, willful.

"How did you happen to become a Zionist?" I asked.

"I was studying medicine. I had no ties to either religion or country. People had always interested me. I felt compassion and pity for all mankind, knowing how everyone shares in illness and joy and grief. But I was restless. All of Europe seemed old and familiar and archaic to me. I was thirsty for something new. And so I came to Palestine."

"Why didn't you go to Russia? They say a new world is being created there . . ."

"Because there's no freedom there. A small, harsh circle governs all the others. The fact that this circle is the proletariat didn't comfort me at all. I wanted freedom."

"And you found it here in Palestine?"

"Here we work free. We try, we experiment, we search to find. You can meet people here and work together according to your individual temperament — from the most revolutionary to the most conservative. Freedom. Here, for the first time, I feel alive, strengthened, able to love the earth that I had never even noticed in Europe, and able to feel joy that I am from the Jewish race."

"You are beginning, in other words, to lose your freedom. You're beginning to tie yourself down to a certain corner of the Earth, and to constrict your heart; first it had room for all the world, now it's beginning to distinguish and choose and to accept only the Jews. Don't you feel the danger?"

The Jewess protested angrily, slightly fearful:

"What danger?"

"What danger? I'll tell you: The leader of the gypsies forbids his people to build houses or plant trees or put up fences. They prop up their tents on the ground for a while and then move on freely. One day, as they were taking down their tents, a young girl was bending over the earth and tarrying. The leader approached and saw the girl had broken his order and had planted a sprig of basil at the entrance of her tent. And now the little sprig of basil had blossomed and the young girl was crouched over it crying, reluctant to leave it. In a rage, the leader uprooted the basil and trampled on it. He struck the girl with his riding whip and shouted: 'Why do you break my order? Don't you know that whoever builds a house is tied to it and whoever plants a tree is tied to that tree?' "

"We don't want to be Wandering Jews any longer!" the Jewess cried out.

"But that is exactly the danger I'm talking about; you don't want to advance any longer. If the purpose of life is happiness — to eat well, to sleep in peace, to live in security — then you are justified in wanting to escape the persecutions and scorn and take roots finally in your own country. Although I'm encouraged by the belief — thank God — that you will not find happiness and security here in Palestine!

"But if the purpose of life, and especially the purpose

178

of a people, is much harder: to struggle to convert as much matter as possible into action, thought and beauty; to climb upward with agony — then, without a doubt, the Zionist movement is contrary to the highest interest of your race."

"Why don't the English or French or Greeks undertake this role of the Wanderer? Or could you possibly think that their contribution to the Whole was lessened because they had a country?"

"Every race has its special virtues and vices and, consequently, its special road to reach its summit. The Jews have this supreme quality: to be restless; not to fit into the reality of the time; to struggle to escape; to consider every status quo and every idea a stifling prison. With this poignant quality of theirs they save mankind from his contrived efforts at contentment — that is to say, from his impasse. This spirit of the Jews shatters the equilibrium, pushes evolution further, sparks off the proudest element of life: never to be satisfied, never to stop anywhere, to leap from plants to animals and from animals to man and again to torment man, as though wanting to go further still."

"Our fathers in the land of Canaan were farmers; rooted to their country they created their civilization."

"That was the nature of your race then. The Jews didn't always have the Lucifer quality of rebellion. They acquired it. The persecutions, slaughters, scorn, exile, all the things you call Diaspora, hammered away at the Hebrew race for two thousand years and forged it, against its will, by force, into the leaven of the earth."

"By force?"

"Does the word annoy you? Isn't it true that force is the most secret law of history? Many races would have

179

wanted to escape their bloody and glorious fate and live
without History, happily — clandestinely. But economic
necessities, wars and some prophets who are born in their
midst don't leave them alone. With force and with the lash,
they prod them upward.

"Thus, scattered over the world for so many centuries,
the Jews suffered, trembled and were killed. And this dyed
their soul indelibly and created in them the hatred for
every tyranny — either from individuals or from systems
or ideas. This is why they agitated nations, undermined
the status quo and set fire to all the old ideas. This is their
fate; without them the world would rot."

Judith laughed.

"Thank you for the role you assign us. I must confess
we are greatly honored to be slaughtered, to be forever
restless, to make others restless. But we don't want to
any more."

"You're tired? But the historical necessity that pushes
the races doesn't ask you. It prods you relentlessly, whether
you want it or not. And this modern Zionist movement,
too, is a mask that your unsmiling Fate wears to deceive
you for an instant. This is why I don't fear Zionism: how
many of the fifteen million Jews will be able to squeeze
themselves in here? You will never find security here. Behind you, don't forget, you have the dark fanatical swarm
of Arabs.

"And so, like it or not, you will become the instruments
of the spirit of our age. And our age is an age of revolution.
That is, a Jewish age. Someone once said: "The twenty-
second of March, 1832, when Goethe died, an era closed
and a new one opened: the era of the reigning of the Jews."
And it's true. Goethe was the last complete representative
of Harmony; after Goethe our contemporary age truly be-

gins — the violence, which is equally valuable, to rupture the old harmony and create a new one. This is why the Hebrew race prevails today, because its substance is precisely this rupturing of every harmony. This is why the highest intellects and leading men of action are Jews. Why all this flowering? Because you are restless, scattered all over the world in a transient age that destroys. Diaspora is your country. In vain you struggle to escape your Fate and you seek out happiness and security in this out-of-the-way province. I hope — I hope, because I love the Jews — that sooner or later the Arabs will drive you out of here and again scatter you all over the world."

We had finally arrived at the children's garden. Blond, brunette and raven-haired Jewish youngsters were playing beneath the trees, chirping away like birds. I caressed their soft curly hair with unexpected emotion; a sudden, tragic foreboding overwhelmed my heart.

CYPRUS

THE ISLE OF
APHRODITE

Cyprus is indeed the native land of Aphrodite. Never have I seen an island with so much fertility or breathed air so saturated with perilous sweet persuasions. In the late afternoon when the sun goes down and the gentle breeze blows in from the sea, soft languor overtakes me — drowsiness and sweetness. And when the small children spill out on the seashore, their hands filled with jasmine, and the little caïques sway lightly in the sea, to right and left, my heart breaks loose and surrenders like the Pandemos[33] Aphrodite.

Here you live incessantly what elsewhere you feel only in rare moments of torpor. You feel it slowly as it penetrates deeply, like the scent of jasmine. "Thought is an effort that goes contrary to the direction of life. The lifting of the soul, the vigilance of the mind, the charge toward the heights, all are the great ancestral sins against the will of God."

The other day while I was still wandering over the mountains of Judea I could hear a contrary relentless cry coming up from the entire land. "Let the hand be severed that it may glorify the Lord. Let the leg be severed that it may dance eternally." The sand trembled and the peaks of the mountains smoldered in the heat of the sun. A harsh god, without water, without a tree, without a woman,

185

walked by, and you could feel the bones in your skull caving in. All of life leaped through the fevered brain like a battle cry.

And now Cyprus reposes in the middle of the open sea, singing softly like a Siren, soothing my troubled head after the abrasive journey through the Judean mountains beyond. We sailed across the narrow sea and in one night passed from Jehovah's camp to the bed of Aphrodite. I was going from Famagusta to Larnaca and from Larnaca to Limassol, all the while getting closer to that holy spot in the sea at Paphos,[34] that fickle, indestructible liquid element in whose foam this feminine mask of mystery was born.

I could clearly feel the two great torrents struggling within me: the one pushes toward harmony, patience and gentleness. It functions with ease, without effort, following only the natural order of things. You throw a stone up high and for a second you force it against its will; but quickly it joyfully falls again. You toss a thought in the air but the thought quickly tires, it becomes impatient in the empty air and falls back to earth and settles with the soil. The other force is, it would seem, contrary to nature. An unbelievable absurdity. It wants to conquer weight, abolish sleep, and, with the lash, prod the Universe upward.

To which of these two forces shall I conform and say: "this is my will," and finally be able with certainty to distinguish good from evil and impose a hierarchy on virtues and passions?

These were my thoughts on the morning I set out from Limassol for Paphos. By noon we were driving through jagged, uninteresting scenery. Carob trees, low mountains, red earth. Now and then a blossoming pomegranate tree unfolded along the way and flickered like flames in the noonday whiteness. Here and there two or three olive trees swayed gently and tamed the landscape.

We passed a dry riverbed blooming with oleander. A small owl was roosting on a stone bridge on the road, motionless, half blinded and paralyzed by the intense light. The landscape was gradually growing gentler. We drove through a village brimming with orchards — the apricots were glimmering like gold on the trees and hulking clusters of loquats shone through the dark thick leaves.

Women began emerging on their doorsteps, plump and heavily dressed. Several men in the coffeehouses turned their heads as we drove by, the others continued their card playing with a passion. A young girl carrying on her shoulder a large round jug that was painted with primitive black designs stepped out of our way, frightened, and took refuge on a large rock. But as I smiled, her face lit up as though the sun shone on it.

The automobile stopped.

"What's your name?" I asked the girl.

I waited for her to say "Aphrodite" but she replied:

"Maria."

"And is Paphos still far from here?"

The girl looked flustered; she didn't understand what I was saying.

"You mean Kouklia,[35] my boy," broke in an old woman. "You mean Kouklia, where you'll find the palace of the Mistress of the Oleanders. It's there, right behind the carob tree."

"And why do they call it Kouklia, ma'am?"

"What? Don't you know? They find dolls there, my boy; little clay women. Here, dig, and you'll find some, too. You're a lord,[36] aren't you?"

"And what do they do with these little women?"

187

"How should I know? Some say they're gods, others say they're devils. Who can tell the difference?"

"What does religion say?"

"What can our poor religion say? Do you think it knows everything?"

The chauffeur was in a hurry so the conversation ended. We passed the village and soon the sea stretched out to our left, again, infinite, deep blue, foamy. And suddenly, as I turned to the right, I saw on the peak of a low hill, far from the road, the ruins of an open, multiwindowed fortress. I knew it was the renowned main temple of Aphrodite. I looked around at the outlines of the mountain, the sea, the small plain where the worshipers must have camped. I tried to isolate this enclave of the much-beloved, full-breasted goddess and relive the vision that once existed here. But, as so often happens to me, my heart was unmoved and unreceptive to all these fleshless fantasies.

The chauffeur stopped in front of a taverna on the road and called out:

"*Kyria*[37] Kalliopi!"

The small door of the taverna opened quickly and the proprietress came out and stood on the doorstep.

I shall never forget her. Tall, full-bodied with ample buttocks, about thirty years old, this smiling, coquettish, earthy, all-enchanting Aphrodite filled the doorway with her presence. The chauffeur looked at her, sighed softly and stroked his youthful moustache.

"Come here," he called. "Are you afraid?"

She laughed and stepped down from her threshold, chuckling. I eagerly cocked my ear to hear the conversation.

"Tomorrow I want you to make me two okas of your best *loukoumia*,"[38] the chauffeur said.

"Twenty-four *grosia*,"[39] answered the woman, sobering. "Nothing less."

"Eighteen."

"Twenty-four."

The man looked at her for a moment; he sighed again. "All right," he said. "Twenty-four? Twenty-four!"

The bargaining ended. The entire landscape took on an unexpected sweetness. This little trifling dialogue had excited my heart. The great temple, all the inspiration of the renowned landscape, the memories, the historical profundity, were unable to move me, but this small human moment resurrected in a flash all of Aphrodite in me.

Thus, joyously, I set out and began the slow climb up the sacred hill.

The thyme, the daffodils, poppies, all the familiar elements one encounters on a Greek mountainside, were there. A young shepherd, goats, sheep dogs, an innocent downy newborn donkey that was frisking about, still looking at the world with surprise.

The sun was finally setting, the shadows were lengthening and touching the earth, the Star of Aphrodite was glittering, playing and twirling in the sky as I entered the deserted temple of the "Mistress." I entered quietly, without excitement, as though I were entering my house. I sat on a rock, thinking of nothing, making no effort at thought. I was gently tired, gently happy, and settled comfortably on the rock. Gradually I began to look at some insects that were chasing each other in the air, intermittently flitting from plant to plant, and I listened to the brittle metallic sound of their wings.

Suddenly, as I was observing the insects, a mysterious fear overtook me. At first I couldn't comprehend the cause, but slowly, with dread, I understood. Engrossed as I was in the insects I remembered, at first dimly, but later more vividly, a frightful sight I had seen in my adolescent years.

One afternoon as I was wandering through a dry river-bed I saw two insects mating under a plane tree leaf. They were two green, willowy, charming little "ponies of the Virgin." I approached them slowly, holding my breath. But suddenly I stopped short, stunned: the male, small and weak, was on top, struggling to consummate its sacred duty; and with horror I saw that its head was missing. The female was calmly chewing it and when she finished she slowly turned and cut off the neck and then she cut off the breast of the male who was clamped tightly over her still pulsating . . .

This terrifying scene suddenly bolted out of the ruins before me. Tonight blue lightning rips through and illumines my heart.

The full-breasted goddess lifts her veil. The breath of the unfathomable is more obvious to plants and animals than it is to man. They, faithful and naked, follow the great Cry. To them, love and death are identical. When we see them headless and chestless, struggling to defeat death by giving birth, we recognize with awe the same Cry within us. The giddiness, the certainty of death; and yet, above this is the joy, the madness in death and the lunge for immortality . . .

It was finally dark. An old man had been watching me from the opposite hill and had come down. He was standing behind me for a long time but did not dare approach but now, as he saw me getting up, he reached out his hand.

"Sir, I've brought you an antique to buy."

He put a small stone in my hand; I looked at it but could not discern what it portrayed. The old man lit a match. Now I could make out the sculptured head of a woman with a war helmet. And as I kept turning the little stone around, I noticed that the upper part of the helmet portrayed the upside-down head of a warrior. I suddenly recalled Ares, and shuddered to see Aphrodite wearing the male thus, as an ornament on her head. I hastily returned the ring stone to the old man.

"Go," I said with involuntary curtness. "I don't like it."

That night I slept at a small hotel nearby. At dawn I had a dream: I was holding a rose, the blackest of roses, in my palm. And as I held it I could feel it slowly, voraciously, silently, eating away at my hand.

NOTES

1. All the books mentioned, with the exception of *Symposium*, are published by Simon & Schuster, New York.
2. *Symposium* (Thomas Y. Crowell, New York, 1975).
3. Eleftherios Venizelos: born in Crete in 1864, died in Paris in 1936. Served as prime minister of Greece from 1910 to 1916, and again from 1928 to 1932. Known as one of the most powerful and influential political leaders in modern Greece. Went into self-exile in 1935 after an unsuccessful coup.
4. Helen Kazantzakis was later to say of this interview that, while her husband was initially impressed with what Mussolini was attempting to do in Italy, he was later to revise his views considerably.
5. *Fellaha*: Kazantzakis uses this word when referring to a female fellah.
6. Yataghan: a long knife or short saber common among Moslems.
7. *Maylahya*: a long rectangular cotton garment, loosely woven in a lacy design, worn over a robe. It is draped about the head, forearms and waist, and ends at the calf.
8. One *oka* is equivalent to 2.82 pounds.
9. Constantine: king of the Hellenes; reigned from 1913 to 1917 and 1920 to 1922.
10. King George of the Hellenes, and his queen, Olga of Russia, whom he married in 1867. They reigned from 1863 to 1913.
11. The hymn to Aton is shown in condensed form, as translated by Kazantzakis.
12. Constantine P. Cavafy (1863–1932): one of the major Greek poets of the century. Born and died in Alexandria.
13. *Mastiha*: an anise-flavored liqueur.

14. See the Cavafy poem "Expecting the Barbarians" (*The Complete Poems by Cavafy*, Harcourt, Brace & World).

15. "The God Forsakes Antony": copyright 1948, by Rae Dalven, from *The Complete Poems of Cavafy*, translated by Rae Dalven, reprinted by permission of Harcourt Brace Jovanovich.

16. *Anagenesis:* the Greek periodical *Renaissance.*

17. *Iconostasis:* the partition in the Greek Orthodox Church that separates the sanctuary from the nave of the church, where the major icons of the church are placed. The *iconostasis* has an opening at the center, called the Holy Gate; the icon of Jesus Christ is always positioned to its right, and to the right of this icon is positioned the icon of John the Baptist. To the left of the gate is the icon of the Virgin Mary, and, to her left, usually an icon of the patron saint of the church. On the two doors to the left and right of the *iconostasis* appear the icons of Archangels Michael and Gabriel.

18. Exodus 3:5.

19. Exodus 3:2.

20. *Epitaphion:* Christ's sepulcher, used in the Holy Week ritual of the Greek Orthodox Church.

21. *Karpenisiotian:* a native of the remote mountain village of Karpenision in mainland Greece; an important battle site during the Greek War of Independence in 1823.

22. *Klephts:* Greek mountain resistance fighters and patriot brigands during the Turkish occupation of Greece, and during the Balkan crises.

23. *Yero:* the Greek word meaning old.

24. Nicephoros Phocas: emperor of Byzantium (963–969 A.D.) and famed general who liberated Crete from the Arabs.

25. Kassiani: a ninth-century Byzantine poet, renowned for her beauty, intelligence and charm. Tradition has it that in 830 A.D. her many virtues captured the heart of Byzantine emperor Theophilos, who wanted to make her his empress. However, in an exchange of conversation, he was both impressed and offended by her brilliance and decided against marrying her. Kassiani later built a monastery, retreated to it and gave herself to religious writing. Among her writings was the renowned "Hymn of Kassiani," a profoundly moving poem which refers to the unknown woman who washed Christ's feet and wiped them with her hair at a dinner at the house of Simon the leper. This stirring hymn is sung on Tuesday of Holy Week in the Greek Orthodox Church.

26. Rabbi Nachman: the founder of the Bratzlaver (Poland) Hasidic sect; great-grandson of Rabbi Israel Baal Shem Tov, founder of Hasidism.

27. *Glykofilusa:* the Virgin of the tender kiss, an icon showing the Virgin wearing a crown, and the Christ child reaching up with his left hand to stroke his mother's chin. Legend has it that this icon escaped destruction during the reign of the Iconoclast, Theophilos, and mysteriously found its way to the Holy Mountain, where it is treasured today.

28. *Apelatiki:* a nail-studded weapon used by frontier guards of the Byzantine Empire.

29. *Yerakokoudouna:* bells of bronze that are found on Cretan lyres.

30. *Tsaprassia:* metal knee plates, worn by Byzantine soldiers, partly for ornament and partly for protection against injury in battle.

31. Prodromos: John the Baptist, the Forerunner of Christ.

32. The Greek word γράμματα refers to alphabetical outlines or letters, and also to education.

33. Pandemos: the earthy goddess of carnal love.

34. Paphos: the ancient city sacred to Aphrodite, on the western tip of Cyprus. There are two cities named Paphos, the old (also called Kouklia) and the new. According to classical legend, old Paphos was founded by Cinyras, who also built the temple of Aphrodite. Aphrodite's birth from sea foam is believed to have occurred at Paphos. According to Hesiod's *Theogony,* Aphrodite was born in the sea, in a circle of white foam created by the mutilated members of Uranus, which had been severed from him by his avenging son, Cronus, and thrown into the sea.

35. Kouklia (or, Ta Kouklia, literally, "the place of the dolls," *koukla* being the Greek word for doll, or a beautiful female) is the new town built on the site of old Paphos, the city sacred to Aphrodite. The region is known for the small clay female figurines that have been excavated.

36. Since Lord Elgin, the villagers, accustomed to English lords excavating their landscape, assumed all strangers interested in antiquities were English lords.

37. *Kyria:* the Greek word for Mrs.

38. *Loukoumi:* a jellylike, gummy confection sprinkled with powdered sugar, known as Turkish delight.

39. *Grosi:* equivalent to about three cents.

ABOUT THE AUTHOR

Nikos Kazantzakis has been acclaimed one of the great writers of our century. His numerous works include novels, dramas, travel journals, poetry, translations, and an important semiautobiographical work, *Report to Greco*. He is best known in this country for his novels, *Zorba the Greek*, *The Greek Passion* (made into the film, *He Who Must Die*), and for his epic poem, *The Odyssey: A Modern Sequel*, a monumental volume of 33,333 lines.

He was born in Crete in 1883, studied law at the University of Athens, where he took a Doctor of Law Degree, and pursued his education in philosophy, literature and art in Germany and Italy. He traveled extensively throughout his lifetime and during brief intervals in Greece served as Greek Minister of Education and as President of the Greek Society of Men of Letters (1945). In 1947–1948 he served as Director of UNESCO's Department of Translations of the Classics.

His work earned him the highest international recognition for literary achievement, including nomination for the Nobel Prize in 1951. He died in Germany in 1957.

ABOUT THE
TRANSLATORS

Themi Vasils has co-translated Nikos Kazantzakis' *Symposium*. She is a contributing script-writer, guest co-producer and hostess to *Everyman*, a weekly television program, on NBC's Channel 5; has written, produced and hosted her own weekly TV program, *The Greek Scene* (1969), and intermittently written, produced and co-hosted other television programs (1965–1969). In preparation: short story translations.

Theodora Vasils has co-translated Nikos Kazantzakis' *Symposium*. Among her translations are short stories by Thanasis Valtinos and Triandafillos Pittas, and a book of poetry, *In Another Light*, by Koralia Theotoka (Ikaros Publishing Co., Athens, 1967). Her work has been published by Harvard University Press and various quarterlies and magazines, including *The Charioteer*, *The Chicago Review*, *The Chicago Sun Times*'s *Midwest Magazine*, *The Literary Review*, and *Poet Lore*. In preparation: the work of the contemporary Greek writer Elli Nezeriti.